LEON TROTSKY:
THE PORTRAIT OF A YOUTH

LEON TROTSKY:
THE PORTRAIT OF A YOUTH

BY
MAX EASTMAN

AMS PRESS, INC.
NEW YORK

Reprinted from the edition of 1925, New York
First AMS EDITION published 1970
Manufactured in the United States of America

International Standard Book Number: 0-404-02235-9

Library of Congress Catalog Card Number: 73-124774

AMS PRESS, INC.
NEW YORK, N.Y. 10003

PREFACE

THE chief thing to be gained by visiting Soviet Russia is a feeling of the characters of the Bolsheviks. To a simple man that makes Bolshevism intelligible. Instead of writing another dissertation about it, therefore, I decided to compose the portrait of one of these characters. I chose Trotsky * because he seems to me the most universally gifted man in the world to-day. There is no one more wholesomely alive, more interested in all the interests of mankind. If we can understand how Trotsky became a Bolshevik, we shall have some human understanding of what Bolshevism is.

For that reason my book is not a record of his achievements, but the story of his youth. I hope to write about those achievements also, but that is a different book. Only remember, while you read, that in 1905, at the age of twenty-six, this Jewish boy, standing at the head of the Petrograd Soviet of Worker's Deputies, spoke with an authority in Russia not inferior to that

* His natal name was Bronstein.

of the czar. The czar's prime minister appealed to that Soviet for the privilege of sending a telegram—and this, while the Soviet was printing and posting in the streets Trotsky's audacious proclamations of its purpose to overthrow the czar's government and establish a socialist state.

Remember that in 1918—untrained even in the contemplation of military affairs—Trotsky organized an army out of the hunger- and panic-stricken remnants of a nation, and fought off on seven fronts an invasion backed up by all the great powers of the world. Remember that he is considered by many who have heard him the greatest orator of our times. And remember that his books of literary criticism, as well as his political and economic studies, are read by every lively-minded man in Russia, and his prose style is a thing of intense individual beauty and power.

I succeeded with some difficulty in persuading Trotsky himself to coöperate with me in composing this story. The degree of his coöperation is described in the following letter.

Dear Comrade Eastman:
 You wish to write my biography and ask my coöperation. My first motion was to refuse that coöperation. But afterward I thought that would be not right.

For better or worse, it befell me to play a certain rôle in the October revolution and its further development. Many people find their way to the *general* through the *personal.* In that sense biographies have their right. And, that being so, better they should be written without great distortions (small ones are quite unavoidable). In this direction—that is, in the direction of conscientious information—I will try to coöperate with you. But I cannot agree to read your manuscript, for that would make me somewhat responsible not only for the factual side, but also for the characterizations and valuations. It is quite obvious that this is impossible. I am ready to take the responsibility and that a limited one, for the facts I communicate in response to your questioning. For all the rest you must bear the responsibility alone.

With sincere greeting,

L. TROTSKY.

To this I ought to add that the facts stated in my concluding chapter about the relation between Lenin and Trotsky in the last years, were none of them supplied to me by Trotsky. These facts are accessible to anybody in Moscow who reads and speaks Russian and stays there a while.

I owe my gratitude for long conversations about Trotsky and his youth to Alexandra Lvovna and Natalia Ivanovna, to Mr. and Mrs. Spencer and their daughter Vera, and to many others who were his playmates and friends. And I owe a more general debt of gratitude to Eliena Vacilievna Krylenko, without whose infinitely generous help all this work in a newly acquired language would have been impossible.

M. E.

Moscow,
May, 1924.

CONTENTS

CHAPTER   PAGE

   I. AN IMPERIOUS SECRETARY . . . 1

  II. A MORAL MATTER 14

 III. A GARDEN OF IDEAS 31

 IV. LOVE AND MARXISM 57

  V. THE WORK AND THE DANGER . . . 79

 VI. SOLITARY CONFINEMENT 98

VII. CONDEMNED TO WRITE 123

VIII. THE SUMMONS OF LENIN 139

 IX. LENIN AND TROTSKY 155

  X. THE BIRTH OF BOLSHEVISM . . . 167

LEON TROTSKY:
THE PORTRAIT OF A YOUTH

CHAPTER I

AN IMPERIOUS SECRETARY

TROTSKY never lived in the big stone house that testifies to the wealth of his parents. He was born and grew up to the age of ten in a little old-fashioned peasant's hut, with a fat brown roof of straw and five tiny rooms with low ceilings. The sitting-room and dining-room had wooden floors, and the floor in the sitting-room was painted; and here there were comfortable chairs, a table, an immense square stove, and on top of the stove a great big sleepy-eyed cat.

In the winter time, when it is impossible to work all day long and all the evening too, his mother sits reading with quiet concentration the words in a book. The process interests him because she whispers the words as she reads. He

1

is cutting out the letters of the alphabet and sticking them fast in the frost on the window, one in each pane, and each little window has six panes. He is sticking them accurately in the middle, you may be sure. It is all snowy white outside, and the drifts curve half way up the low windows, and it is all warm inside, and tender and friendly and unworried.

The elder brother and sister will explain to him about the letters and give him his first colored books to read. And then when they are gone away to school he will be taken over to an aunt's house in the village, and he will stay there studying with her children. Nominally he will stay all winter, but as a matter of fact he will be at home most of the time, because he is so sweet-tempered and has such merry dimples that his parents cannot get along without him. In the summers an uncle from Odessa will come to visit them, and he too will give lessons to this gifted child with the beautiful manners and the blue light shining out of his eyes. Everybody who sees him will help him, and he will have every opportunity to rise to a place of respectability and comparative honor in Russian society.

And he will avail himself of these opportunities with a speed the memory of which makes people breathless. By the time that you might have learned to make letters with a pen, Trotsky had lost interest in the letters and was making a pen. At the age of eight he was printing with his pen a little magazine—although this with the help of a cousin two years older, a great artist, who made the cover designs. Trotsky's first ambition was to be a great artist like his cousin. And his first job was to be, at the age of seven, his father's secretary and account-keeper, a job which he fulfilled with an accuracy and perfection of penmanship entirely beyond the reach of his elder brother and sister.

Trotsky never played very much out of doors. He never learned to skate, and he can swim only a little. His early friends describe him as a "mischievous" child, but they do not mean that he went around with bow and arrows and a sling-shot, spit-balls and cigarette-butts, sticking burrs in the lambs' tails and riding the cows bareback. They refer to what he said rather than to what he did. His friendship was full of laughter; he liked personal jokes, and had ironical-affectionate ways of appreciating people. The nearest he came to playing, in our sense, was to "hang around" his father's machine-shop and blow the bellows or turn the wheels for his best friend, Grebin, the farm mechanic, with whom his conversations were endlessly lively and adventurous. He remembers, when he was seven years old, talking of the improbability of people's going up in the sky somewhere after they die. But that too was a playful conversation. He can not remember caring much whether they went up there or not. He can not remember ever having a serious emotion in regard to the religion about which his parents tried to tell him a little. His seriousness was bent from the beginning in a different direction.

It would be interesting to understand, if we could, just why this happy and healthy-natured child—a miracle of brain and will-power, as everybody could see—did *not* rise to a position of respectability and comparative honor in Russian society. Instead he crawled under Russian society, disreputable and like dynamite; and only because of the whole of that society toppled and fell, he rose to his position of honor.

It appears that the fact of his being a Jew had little influence in the formation of Trotsky's character and destiny. It was of course an objective limitation of the things that were pos-

sible to him under the czar, but it was not a thing
that entered into his heart in childhood. His
father had belonged to a community of Jewish
people—"colonists," who took up free land
under an edict of the czars designed to increase
the population of southern Russia.

But while the others all stayed in the colony,
hating the land and satisfied with small trade,
his father moved out into the fields and got rich
working and hiring the peasants to work with
him. He controlled almost three thousand acres
of land around the little Ukrainian village of
Ianovka, owned the mill, and was altogether the
important man of the place. Trotsky had no
chance to develop an "inferiority complex" here.

And he received his early education in Odessa,
a sea-port trading city, where commercial necessity disciplined the races, Greeks and Jews and
Russians, and their relations were in normal
times courteous, at least, and not constrained.
Unfriendly allusions to his race were "merely
another kind of rudeness"; they were not one
of the things he cried about. And they have left
no traces apparently in his consciousness of himself. Trotsky has the bearing and the manner
toward life of a prince, if you can imagine that
nature has her princes, and nothing seems more

remote and petty in his presence than the distinctions of race.

It was from his father that Trotsky inherited the most obvious traits of his endowment, the intellect, the confident and penetrating judgment. His father died in a little village near Moscow four years ago at the age of eighty-three. He was managing a mill with energy and success, and he died not of old age, but of typhus fever.

A strong man who had been wealthy, who had been respected with a good deal of fear by his neighbors, he found himself at the age of eighty —thanks to his obstreperous son—in the most uncomforted condition of any man in Russia. Persecuted by the Reds because he was a *kulak,* a big land-grabber, by the Whites because he was Trotsky's father, and by Machno's bandits on the general theory that he might have something that they wanted, he got the full weight of the "Russian problem."

He thought it over under those circumstances and read it over a little too—for he had learned to read at the age of sixty—and finally gave up the faith of a lifetime and left home. He went three hundred miles through battle-ridden territory on foot—eighty years old—seeking a friend with whom he could take shelter, and in 1920 he arrived in Moscow, reconciled to the revolution and glad to ask his errant son for a job.

Trotsky is proud of his father, proud of the fact that he died working and understanding. He loves to talk about him.

His memory of his mother is less affectionate. I think it is because he loved her too much when he was a child. But perhaps it is only because she died longer ago, and Trotsky never lived much with his family.

He went away to school at the age of nine, and very soon after that he began living in jail. He remembers both his parents as they came to see him in the little cell in the prison at Odessa. It was a very tiny barred shaft into which he had been admitted only for the purpose of the visit; but when they saw him there with his big black mane and gentle eyes, like a wild animal in a cage, they did not understand. They believed that he was kept in that cage to protect the czar's domains from the rage of his terrible ideas.

His father expressed no feeling, but turned white and had to support himself against the wall. But his mother's anger and pain expressed themselves violently. She had not so much of

the reserve that Trotsky loves, and that gives to
his presence an exciting quality of power. She
had the power, however. Her neighbors remember that she was an "insistent" character,
and a "great manager," and that the Bronsteins'
estate was as efficiently run, and their household
as spick and span and punctual to its dates, as
the famous military train of the Commander-
in-Chief of the Red Armies. They remember
that she was a handsome woman, with "a face
full of goodness," and that neither she nor her
husband was "the kind to sit down in front of
any kind of *work*."

So far there is no reason to see why Trotsky
should not become a "regular person" and go
serenely upward to that respectable position
which his parents desired for him. But there
was a difference between them. Trotsky was in
the first place an extremely intense and sensitive
child. He seemed to "care too much" about
things. There never was a child born who had
less of the disposition to "let well enough alone."
And the things he cared about were unusual.

One day a neighbor's horse broke into his
father's wheat-field. The neighbors' horses were
always breaking into his father's fields. His
father had so many fields. And perhaps it

wasn't just the horses who were so clever. At any rate his father was very severe in the administration of justice on these occasions. He locked the horse up, and told the peasant he would let him out when the damages were paid.

Trotsky saw his father striding back into the house and the poor peasant coming after him with his hat in his hand, crying:

"I didn't see him, it wasn't my fault! I didn't see him, it wasn't my fault!"—bent over as though he were a little old woman who needed help.

Trotsky ran into his mother's bedroom and into the bed by the window. He lay there curled up on the blanket, crying. It was dark, and it was dinner-time, but he did not answer when they called him to dinner. He felt all the sorrow in the world then, and he looked out of the window in the dark. His mother finally got up from the table to look for him, calling out of both doors and receiving no answer. She found him at last. Perhaps he let her hear a sob from the bedroom. But she came back without him.

"That's a queer child," she said. "He's been crying for a half an hour, and I don't know what he's crying about."

His father was more understanding.

"I think he heard Ivan wailing about that horse," he said. "Tell him Ivan has the horse, and he didn't pay anything."

So Trotsky found himself in the embarrassing position of having to stop crying suddenly because he had made a mistake. He managed it by denying that he had been crying about Ivan's horse, and coming up to the table snuffling and pouting in a solemn way, as though he had been communing with some sorrow too deep for grown-up people to understand.

He probably had been communing with a deeper sorrow—but perhaps we can dimly understand it if we try. Trotsky was devotedly attached to his mother in those early days. His relation with his father—according to the testimony of one who lived often in their house—was "none too cordial." That must have been the fundamental fact in his emotional life, and it is easy to imagine that some egotistical and jealous pains of his own were mixed up with his sympathy for that unhappy peasant. The deepest and tenderest passion in his heart led him into a mood of rebellion against the dominance of his father. And that mood was more or less continual. It got him into trouble more than once.

Trotsky was a most extraordinary secretary. Sitting there with his big blank books, a big ink-well and pen, a big shock of darkening hair, but everything else about him incredibly small, his legs reaching only halfway down to the floor, he had nevertheless a very important, rapid and solemnly competent manner of doing what had to be done—changing and dealing out money, noting down the amounts paid and the amounts received. On pay-days he was especially busy, for his father had a mill and a threshing-engine on his big farm, and many different kinds of laborers. And here again there would be disputes—particularly with the season workers, who were compelled to pay for damage to property and for the days when they were ill.

You can imagine his father's emotion when in the midst of one of these disputes his small and perfect secretary suddenly stepped in with the announcement that he had computed the amount remaining to the worker, and it was not enough to get along on. He would have to have more. This was offered simply as a statement of fact. But as it seemed not altogether obvious to his father, it was backed up with something approaching the nature of a speech for the opposition, a thing exceedingly *mal-à-propos* in a seven-year-old secretary. An intolerable thing in fact. His father told him to "shut up," and that was the end of it.

It was in this manner that Trotsky varied from the conventional type and became such a care and disappointment to his well-regulated parents. His sympathies were belligerent. His tenderness was rebellious. He seemed to have an idea arising out of himself as to how things ought to be, and little or no discretion about expressing it.

His father thought that this cantankerous streak in his gifted son would disappear with proper education. He had unbounded faith in Leon's abilities, and he had vast and exciting ambitions for him. He used to exhibit his little magazine to everybody who came into the house —and also his colored drawings, of which Trotsky made enough to fill a hay-mow, all neat and accurate in perspective and without a glimmer of artistic value. And he used to call upon Leon to recite his "poetry"—of which he also poured out an unconscionable stream, for some reason that is beyond understanding. For Leon's poetry had nothing in it, neither music nor images nor emotion, and he himself had no disposition to show it off. In fact he rebelled violently against these exhibitions, dug his fingers in his eyes, crawled around behind the furniture, and on one occasion when a little girl from the neighboring farm had been called in to hear him, he just burst out yelling in the middle of a poem and ran away and hid in the barn.

He was a queer child from the standpoint of an ambitious parent—too sensitive, and yet too obstreperous. But he had brains, he had health, he had energy. The thing to do was to put him to school, and put him to school early. An uncle in Odessa—Spencer—the same one who had given him lessons in the summer months—offered to take Leon into his home as a "paying guest." He could live there in a cultivated family and attend the St. Paul's School, the best boys' school in Odessa.

CHAPTER II

THUS at the age of nine Trotsky arrived in a new home with new parents to take care of him—to try, that is, to keep him from studying too hard and rocking the baby to death. For these were apparently his two principal bad habits. The baby was only three weeks old when he arrived in the house, and he watched over her development with intense affection. He detected her first smile, he taught her to walk, he taught her to read.

She is a gay and lively young woman now, studying dramatic art in Moscow and cherishing like jewels the memory of his friendship and the little shreds of his letters that used to come to her from Siberia, torn and blotted by the czar's censor. Her mother and father are still living, too—kindly-quiet, poised, intelligent. You can hardly imagine a more wholesomely peaceful environment for this boy of too intense mental energy, who cared too intensely about having things right.

14

To the mother his coming to their home was like turning on a light. She can only tell you how his eyes shone, and how beautiful he was, and polite, and terribly clean, and always busy, and always merry, and how all the teachers in their school loved him, and everybody loved him. And if you ask her, just for the sake of the picture, to put in a little of the darker color, she will answer:

"I never saw him rude and I never saw him angry in my life. The worst trouble I had was that he was so terribly neat. I remember once he had a new suit, and we went out walking, and all the way he kept picking imaginary lint off that suit. I said to him, 'If you do that everybody will know that you have on a new suit.' But it made no difference. He had to have everything perfect.

"That is why he stood so high in drawing. The first time he brought me a sketch to show me, it was so accurate and complete that I thought it was one they had given him to copy. But then he always stood at the top of the class in everything. He would always get hold of other books besides the ones they were supposed to study out of, and then he would read all about a subject, and most of the teachers would skip him when they were asking questions, for fear he would tell them something they didn't know.

"There was one teacher there who never would give a mark of five. 'Only God gets five!' he used to say. But he gave Leon five—he simply had to. Another boy tried his best to get that mark, but the teacher told him again, 'I don't give fives.'

" 'You gave Bronstein five!' the boy said.

" 'That's Bronstein!' the teacher answered."

It is a relief to know that Trotsky committed at least one sin in those days. He abstracted a few of Mr. Spencer's best books from the book-case and sold them to buy candy. He did not want the candy, either; it was worse than that; he just wanted to take the books. That gave him a great feeling of independence. He remembers standing in a doorway a little way down the street, eating that candy rapidly and laboriously, as one gets rid of the unpleasant consequences of an indulgence.

In general, however, his life there in Odessa seemed to have been as virtuous and serene as Mrs. Spencer's happy memory of it. Mr. Spencer remembers that this serenity was in part the result of a personal reserve extraordinary in so young a child.

"We did not really know what Leon was thinking about," he said. "I can only tell you certainly two things: That during that time he had no interest in girls, and he had no interest in sports. He was a very clever child—not only in his books—but he was tactful. He knew that he had come into a strange family, and he knew how to behave. He was only ten years old, but he was self-contained and self-confident. And he had an extraordinary sense of duty that must have been instinctive. No one had to take charge of his training, no one had to worry about his lessons. He always did more than was expected of him."

To this somewhat appalling perfection of Trotsky, as reported by teachers, guardians and the like admiring elders, must be added the further appalling fact that he liked it. He liked to excel everybody. It was not the pure thirst of knowledge that brought him those high marks; it was a thirst of high marks. Indeed he was not even content to excel his school-mates, but he would go and think up impossible questions that he knew even the teachers could not cope with, and then when they floundered hopelessly he very politely suggested the answer.

The Russians, whose language often shows a

better psychology than ours, have a special word for this quality, distinguishing it on the one hand from ambition, and on the other hand from self-conceit. Trotsky had at this time no particular ambition, and he could not at any time be called conceited. He was exceedingly *samoliubív,* and you will have to know what that word means if you want to understand him and appreciate the difficulties that he must have had, or life had, in disciplining his nature. It means a fierce eagerness to excel others, and an intemperate sensitiveness to a challenge, or to the presence of a challenging personality.

It is that set of electric springs in the nervous system which we cultivate by selective breeding in race-horses, and which might be called in English an instinct for rivalry. It makes them, you know, even when they are ambling along at a resting pace, keep at least one white eye backward along the track to see if there is anything in the field that considers itself an equal. It involves an alert awareness of self, and is upon the whole a very disagreeable trait—especially as it appears to those horses who were not bred for speed.

It is something of a problem, in view of these facts, to know why Trotsky was so well loved

as he was by his playmates. I can not find anyone who will say that he stood apart because of
his superior ability. He was a popular boy in
school.

"Even the boys in the upper class," said one
of them, "knew that in the first class there was
this little boy, Leon Bronstein."

It was not because of any heroism on the play-
ground; Trotsky's genius for excelling did not
seem to function here. He did not play much—
in all his seven years in Odessa he never went
rowing with the boys on the bay. And he was
not much of a fighter either.

His first arrival in the school was signalized
by an event very little suggesting the future
commander of an army. He was all dressed up
in a brand-new uniform—and Trotsky loves to
be dressed up; he loves gloves and shapely cos-
tumes—all those things that are supposed to be
incompatible with revolution. His uniform had
yellow buttons and a yellow buckle at the belt
and a cap with a blue peak and crossed golden
palm-leaves with letters signifying the "St.
Paul's School of Odessa."

"Those yellow buttons afforded me an inde-
scribable delight," he told me, "and in general
it seemed to me that upon my shoulders, or at

least in my knapsack, rested the dignity of the whole school whose threshold I was about to cross for the first time. I advanced, I imagine, with majestic solemnity. There came to meet me one of the so-called 'street boys,' most likely a pupil from a work-shop—fourteen years old, if not more. I was nine.

"As we met, he stood still, looked me over from head to foot, cleared his throat deeply and spat on my sleeve. That was as unexpected as if a burnt-out meteor had fallen on me from a clear sky. Especially it seemed incomprehensible to me, that he could spit on that magnificent brand-new costume, which signified so profound a turning-point in my existence. After a complete stupefaction which lasted several seconds—the boy meanwhile going away to his friends—I began to wipe off the shameful spot with chestnut leaves. To my offender I said never a word—in the main, I judge, through utter bewilderment, but perhaps in part also through awe before a being to whom nothing in the world was sacred.

"I understand him better now, I must confess, and in some sense sympathize with him. That wild spit was a form of protest for his dirty and degraded childhood."

Trotsky was not much of a fighter in the school-boy sense, but he was absolutely without fear. And that rare union of sensitive sympathy with imperious force, which so distressed his father, must have endeared him to his companions. They all remember one famous incident of his eleventh year, which sums up his character for them. They all remember it differently, but I think I have found out the true story.

One evening Leon, the happy, the strong-hearted, came home from school quivering and sobbing wildly. He could hardly say what had happened to him. Mrs. Spencer to this day does not know exactly what happened. He could only gasp:

"I don't want to be expelled! What will my papa say, if I am expelled from school!"

And he would not be consoled, though she and her husband promised to see the principal, and assured him that he would be taken back after everything was straightened out and explained. He felt that nothing could be straightened out, that nothing could be explained.

This is what had happened. A boy named Vakker, who was the son of the cook in a teacher's family, was a very stupid boy, who had already been two years in the same class. If he had to stay in that class another year he would be automatically dismissed from the school. A teacher named Gustave Burnand was a very priggish and unamiable teacher, with a big scar on his forehead and a thin, mean face lengthened with a little piece of a beard. Burnand gave Vakker so low a mark in his course that it was evident he could not pass out of the second class that year, and Vakker sat there almost all day crying.

Leon organized a protest. That was his crime—he *organized*. It was a very elementary sort of protest, but it was well organized and came off splendidly. When Burnand turned his back to go out of the room after the lesson, his exit was welcomed with a loud and prolonged "boo!" from the entire class. He wheeled around with an indignant glare, but all was still and respectful. He glared long enough to appall the most unruly, and then turned again. The "boo!" was repeated, a little feebler, but it followed him all the way down the hall.

Vakker, however, still was sitting in the corner crying, and it seemed as if nothing substantial had been accomplished. So Trotsky proposed a further measure of protest. He thought up the name of a very lofty official—something like the President of the State Board of Education—and proposed that they should write him a letter on the urgent need for rectification in the conduct of the second class in French in the St. Paul School.

"But we would be expelled from school!" the other boys said.

"We will each write one letter of each word," he answered, "and they won't be able to say who did it. They can't expel us all."

In the midst of this more elaborate conspiracy on behalf of the oppressed, Professor Burnand appeared in the doorway with the principal of the school. They had come to ascertain the primary source of this booing, and they opened their investigation by dragging the oppressed himself out of his corner and inquiring what he had to do with it.

"It wasn't me," he wailed, pointing tearfully at the champion of his rights. "It was Leon done it!"

So Leon was invited to remain after school, and please to appear at four o'clock in the office of the principal. He remembers vividly the scene in that holy-of-holies from which no sinner returns unrepentant. He remembers the old

priestly-ferocious German who conducted the
school, and who was to give him his sentence of
expulsion. He remembers the prim and exalted
attitude of his accuser, and how as he entered
tremulously the awful chamber this man announced with an inflection meant to wither the
bones of the guilty:

*"The first boy in my class is a Moral Mon-
ster!"*

Mrs. Spencer put on her bonnet and coat and
appeared early in that office the next morning
to know why her boy should be expelled from
school.

"Bronstein!" said the old German. "You
want us to take that boy back? Let me tell you
that's a bad boy. He has all the boys in the
school under his power. That boy is going to
be a dangerous member of society. We don't
want him here."

"How can you say that about a child eleven
years old!" said Mrs. Spencer.

"Madam, I have an experienced eye. I tell
you that when that boy grows up he will be
dangerous."

"But you have no right to deprive such a brilliant child of an education."

"Oh, he is brilliant all right. That's just the

trouble." The old man was relenting a little. "I'll tell you how much I'll do. I'll bring this matter up again before the faculty council; let them decide."

So Mrs. Spencer took her way to everyone of Trotsky's teachers, and from all but one she received the same answer:

"He is the pride of the school—we will do everything in our power to keep him here."

So early the disagreement began!

The old man did have an experienced eye. And Burnand, too, was not without a poetic felicity in his choice of epithets. The thing that makes Trotsky's moral arrogance seem monstrous is that it sleeps in the breast of so gracious a person. The Communists have agreed in large part with the rest of the world in picturing their military hero as a nervous, proud Satanic rebel, wearing a perpetual ironic scowl. But Trotsky is distinguished in an ordinary public assembly by his serene composure. His head held high, but his body solid and without nervous movement, he conveys an impression of alert and childlike quietude. What you see in his blue eyes is goodness; his mouth is sensuous and happy in its curve; and there is always the readiness for a social dimple in his cheek. If you add to these engaging qualities, extreme youth, a long-suffering attentiveness in the class-room, and a silent, diligent accuracy in doing the work, you will understand with what sincere horror a teacher might behold those dimples harden into iron ruts, those blue eyes shoot light-ning, and some perfectly intolerable insolence come out of that mouth.

Trotsky's absorbing interest as a student in those days was history. He read the text-books of history at school, and then he read all the books about history that he could find in the Spencers' library. He read the Bible as history.

It had been an ambition of his father's—as combining cultural elevation with a certain con-ventional piety—to have a private tutor read the Bible with his son in the original Hebrew. Trotsky, being only eleven years old, was some-what abashed before the bearded old scholar who undertook this task. And the scholar, being old and full of his duty, was hesitant about un-veiling his own critical views to so young a boy. So it was not quite clear at first whether they were reading the Bible as history and literature, or as the revealed word of God. Trotsky re-marked one day, in a reconnoitering spirit:

"I heard some people say that there is no God, and I asked them:

" 'How, then, can you explain the existence of the world?'

"It was too much for the self-restraint of an old agnostic, who answered:

" 'Yes, but after you have explained the existence of the world by means of God, by what means then will you explain the existence of God?' "

After that an intellectual friendship was established, and Trotsky was the more encouraged in the development of his own extremely positivistic mind.

In the later years his interest turned from history to mathematics as the chief concern. But all through these school-days—and indeed all through his life—Trotsky has had an interior thirst after literature and literary creation—a feeling that he cannot possibly know enough or attain enough in this field, that is restless and not happy. It is the wistfulness of a born man of action—the reverse of Hamlet's wistfulness. And it makes him the most indefatigable buyer of books in the whole world.

"If they would just let me come back to Paris

once more," he said to me, "and wander along the banks of the Seine, selling my old clothes to buy books!"

It was this thirst that brought Trotsky again in the sixth year into conflict with the law and order of the school. His teacher up to that time, in literature and the Russian language, had been a sincere lover of his subject and of the art of teaching. He had encouraged the boys in founding a little magazine for their compositions—had encouraged Trotsky in particular, after the appearance of the first number, to study the laws of meter before he wrote any more poetry.

Upon graduating into the sixth class Trotsky came into the hands of another teacher of composition, a lazy man who cared little about composition and nothing about teaching. This man could simply never get around to the point of correcting the papers. Trotsky would labor through forty books gathering material for an essay, and then write the essay not with a pen, but with a sharp flame—such eagerness, such mental and manual energy and exactitude. And then he would hand it in to his teacher and never hear of it again. It was like dropping jewels into a well.

Trotsky decided to organize. One morning

when the teacher had announced for the fiftieth time that he would return their papers the next day and was proceeding to give out the subjects for a new composition, he was startled to hear from the first boy addressed a weak but valiant announcement:

"I won't write the new composition until after you correct my last one."

"Keep still! What do you mean?" said the teacher.

"Well, you ought to correct our papers," murmured the boy, looking around helplessly for support.

"You may leave the room," was the answer. And Trotsky felt his organization crumbling. He jumped to his feet.

"He is entirely right," he said. "You will have to correct our first papers before you ask us to write a second!"

It was the voice of command. I have noticed that voice, and I am not surprised at what happened. It is deep, but it is not a big, liquid, luminous sound like Chaliapin's. There is an electric crackle in it. You feel when you are talking to Trotsky a little bit as though you were doing something dangerous.

The teacher walked out of the room. Trotsky

was sixteen years old, and his popularity and mental brilliance had given him a rather formidable character. The other boy was expelled for insubordination, but Trotsky—on the ground that he had already been expelled once!—was sentenced to twenty-four hours of solitary confinement.

He was locked up, but his former teacher, the good friend of his poetry, was now the "inspector" of the school. He came to talk with the culprit several times during the day, and at nightfall secretly unlocked the door and sent him home.

After that the compositions were corrected. And our moral monster succeeded in graduating from the St. Paul's School without further alarming the experienced eye and vegetative soul of its management. He left behind him, indeed, a glow of personal affection and intellectual glory which never entirely died out to this day, when the boys of the working-classes of Odessa go there to receive a free education in the "School of the Name of Comrade Trotsky."

CHAPTER III

A GARDEN OF IDEAS

THERE was no seventh class in the St. Paul's School in Odessa, so the boys were accustomed to go from there to another school in the same city. But because it was nearer to his lonely parents, Trotsky decided to finish his course in the smaller city of Nikolaev, a night's ride by steamboat down the coast from Odessa.

Here his father engaged a comfortable lodging for him, and here he arrived in the autumn of 1895, wearing a nicely pressed new suit of a rich tan color, his hair cropped short and a stylish hat on his head, very handsome, very bourgeois—according to those who offered him the lodging—and almost a bit of a swell. It is not quite true that he "had no interest in girls." He was very shy in his relations with girls and disposed when he was particularly interested in one to cover it up or express it by treating her with special rudeness and brutality—a method which did not get him along very fast. But he had a great love of social laughter and a boisterous good time and enjoyed the advantages of his good looks like any other boy excited about life.

Inwardly he was not quite so slick and cocksure, however, as he appeared. He was troubled about himself in two respects. He had an ambitious impulse toward knowledge and literary expression, and he had a perpetual sense of the impossibility of ever satisfying it. He lay awake at night, troubled about this. He did not know what he was going to do; he thought he would earn his living as a mathematician or an engineer.

The other thing that troubled him was an inability to make decisions. He thought that his will was sickly. He seemed to be perpetually going around in a desperate circle, considering the pros and cons of every little movement and doing nothing. He did not see how he could ever play the part of a man with this moral impediment!

Trotsky says that he still finds it difficult to make decisions in small matters. Perhaps it is choices, rather than decisions, that he finds difficult. In those days in Nikolaev and even in the great matters he had not chosen his goal. He had no calling, and he had no love.

He was a republican in feeling. He loved the victories of the people in history and hated their slavery in Russia to the czar. But he had not yet touched that dark current of political change that had been gathering power in his country for half a century. Two men brought him in contact with it—one, Franz Svigofsky, a thoughtful gardener; the other Galatsky, a book-seller. In czarist Russia all book-sellers were radical —to sell books was a radical occupation—and this book-seller leaned to the left even among his own adventurous kind. He gave Trotsky radical pamphlets and rational-idealistic books to read, like Lavrov's "Historic Letters" and Michaelovsky's "What Is Progress?"—books which painted a Socialist ideal and warmly glorified the lives of those who should devote themselves to its attainment.

These were among the first books in Russia which proposed a revolutionary social evangel in the place of the religious evangel which has absorbed so much of the aspiration of mankind. They advocated a "going to the people" on the part of young men and women who had the advantage of education and wished to further the progress of the race. The peasants are the people, they said; go and live among the peasants in the villages; teach them all that you know; but teach them particularly about Socialism and about the advisability of overthrowing the czar, if necessary, in order to establish a Socialist society.

In these books, written in a very noble and elevated style, Trotsky found a common channel for many of the prevailing currents in his nature. Without offending his hard sense of reality they offered him an ideal. They offered him the world as a field for that instinct toward "having things right" which was so strong in him.

There is a terrible seriousness in people to whom religion seems trivial. And these books showed Trotsky how he might live life seriously, and with a goal greater than himself and his daily bread and bootblacking. They showed him the glory of the adventure of human progress. And they gave him companionship in those peculiarly strong feelings of social sympathy and revolt which he had brought with him out of his childhood. He felt that he belonged to this company of reasonable and devout rebels of human progress.

In this mood it was inevitable that he should come in contact with a group of bold and radical-minded and excessively noble-minded young people, who met in the outskirts of the town in the garden of Comrade Franz Svigofsky. Comrade Svigofsky's brother was in the high-school with Trotsky, and he already called himself a *Narodnik*—a believer, that is, in "the people" and in "going to the people."

And Comrade Svigofsky himself, while not exactly a *Narodnik*—not quite so revolutionary as that name implied—was a man of broad and free culture, who had gathered around himself by a kind of natural gravitation everybody in the town who had a radical opinion. A gardener by trade, he had leased this plot of ground, and was trying to make an independent living raising fruit and vegetables. His little house, however, had a comfortable dining-room and an open arbor under an apple tree where you could sit around the samovar and talk about the possibilities of perfecting human society; and it was always full of *Narodniki* and *Narodovoltsi* and *Narodopravtsi;* and even now and then a Marxist would creep in, and it is to be feared that the fruit and vegetables led a very precarious life among all these high-minded people. At any rate Comrade Svigofsky's garden was better known to the police than it was to the green-goods merchants of Nikolaev; and when the news reached Trotsky's parents that he was "hanging around" this notorious place a very tempestuous situation developed.

His father invaded Nikolaev like an army. He fell upon Trotsky, and he fell upon the poor woman who kept the lodging where Trotsky lived, and who, he thought, should have had some regard for a young man's development. His son was to have a course in civil engineering at St. Petersburg or, if he preferred it, an education abroad. There was to be no nonsense about it. There was money enough in the family to produce something besides a radical ne'er-do-weel for a son!

Trotsky was not sure that he would not study engineering; but he was sure that he would not let anybody else choose his life for him, and he said so.

The conflict that ensued was sharp and rude and cruel. The will that had built up that great estate and personality in spite of illiteracy and the disadvantage of race had projected itself forward into this incomparable son. The farm was not enough—sugar-mills and breweries were to be built now—an engineer was indispensable.

The son, on the other hand, was far away from building sugar-mills and breweries. He was organizing the people who dropped in at Svigofsky's garden into a little society, which he took a poetic pleasure in calling the *Razsadnik*. It means a garden in which things are grown for the purpose of transplantation. And the things to be grown in this garden were revolutionary ideas. The members met every week or so to discuss the problem of the liberation of Russia and the regeneration of human life, and they paid each a certain proportion of his income, to be used in buying books for distribution among the peasants. It was only a "little circle of intellectuals"—but it was a typical forerunner of the events to come, a small forge in which instruments were being sharpened for the use of the great forces of history. And to Trotsky, who believed then that these instruments *were* the great forces of history, it was of more pressing importance than his hypothetical career as a civil engineer. He said this to his father, and he said it with a sharp and violent tongue.

His father knew nothing about defeat.

"You will either quit this business and get to work, or you will quit spending my money," was his ultimatum.

If any last touch was needed to drive Trotsky

straight into the camp of the revolution, it was this act of paternal tyranny. His revolt against his father and his revolt against the social system now became united. To assert himself as a grown man was to assert the revolution. He made no remonstrance against the terms of the ultimatum. He gave up the lodging that had been rented for him, advertised himself as a private tutor and moved over to Svigofsky's garden to live.

The incident has repeated itself in Trotsky's own family. His eldest boy, having decided that the privileges of life in the Kremlin as the son of a Commissar are not befitting his dignity as an individual, has moved out into the town and lives there upon the small stipend provided by the university to its students. He visits his family once a week as a guest, refusing to accept even his car-fare when he leaves the house. He is only sixteen years old, and it was with a mixture of admiration and solicitude that Trotsky told me about it.

"We have made no protest," he said; "but it is too early—he is too young."

Trotsky was too young—he was just past sixteen. He had come to Nikolaev only in order to be near his family. He had no clear or defined purpose in life except to live it. It was a hard moment for his affections. But it was not altogether hard, for the world into which he had cast himself was warm and full of friends. Indeed, it was almost an ideal world. Franz Svigofsky was a simple and most genial man, a man with a big beard and a big brow, and his relation with this brood of young rebels that surrounded him was that of an appreciative but prudent father. Together they had established in that garden a kind of Communal Utopia— he and his brother and the two Sokolovsky brothers, and in the summer-time a Doctor Zif who was studying medicine at Kiev.

Doctor Zif had a home in Nikolaev, but he was very fond of the Svigofskys, and particularly he loved Trotsky, and you could almost say that he lived there in the garden. By taking turns at the cooking and dishwashing, and with the very important help of Svigofsky's long-suffering vegetables, these five or six friends managed to enjoy the best pleasures of human society at the modest rate of eleven rubles apiece per month.

And Trotsky's income as a "private tutor" sometimes amounted to eleven rubles a month, although it was the most uncertain thing in the world. At one time he managed to rope in the son of a local dry-goods merchant and filled him so full of unnecessary knowledge that at the end of two months his father, taking fright at the boy's development, refused to pay the bill.

There could hardly have been a more unlikely location for a private tutor of Nikolaev's wealthy sons than Comrade Svigofsky's garden. And there could hardly have been a more inauspicious regalia than the blue workman's blouse, the wild-growing hair and the cane of a special form which had been "standardized" by the habitués of that nest of liberality and sedition.

The truth is that Trotsky immediately accepted a real and complete poverty as a part of the choice that he was making. When he did earn money he did not spend it on himself. He gave up all those attributes, except fastidious cleanness, of the slick young man who had arrived in Nikolaev a half a year ago. He was no less gay and humorsome, but he had turned to a new life; and he lacks the capacity for half-hearted action. He is described as "ragged" by his bourgeois friends during the two years that he lived and worked for Socialism in Nikolaev and Odessa, and he was often actually hungry for a meal.

His uncle, Spencer, remembers a morning when Trotsky appeared in front of his office window in Odessa, gaunt and ill-clad as a tramp. Spencer jumped up, shocked and startled, intending to open the door, but Trotsky beckoned him to come out and meet him a little way down the street.

"It was not because he was ashamed of his tattered clothes," Mr. Spencer explained, "but because he was doing illegal work then and did not want to involve me. I took him to a restaurant and bought him a breakfast, and then another breakfast, and then another breakfast, before I could get him filled up."

Trotsky remembers another time, however, when his income as a teacher amounted to sixty rubles a month, and then he was the rich one in the garden. He was the one who had money left over to buy books for the peasants!

Such was their life. And the heart of it—the sustaining joy and justification of it—was a relentless, exhaustive, young, brilliant, burning, day-long and night-long debate on the problems of the social revolution in Russia.

It is impossible for us in America to imagine with what intense realism the idea of a more perfect human society was conceived in Russia,

and with what sheer practicality its problems
were discussed. To us Socialism came as a
gratuitous economic vagary, requiring a philosophic dissatisfaction with the forms of democracy, and proposing a kind of ideal uprising that
had as little reality for our lives as the second
coming of Christ. To the Russians an ideal
uprising was inevitable. Everybody expected it.
The czar expected it. And everybody knew
that this uprising would destroy, if successful,
the most sanctified relations between the classes
in Russian society. What set of relations should
take their place? That was a simple and practical question that every lively-minded person
must ask. Socialism was one of the answers.
It was the answer given by the most thoughtful,
and also by the most thoughtless. Only a certain mildly intellectual or dull professorial type
of person believed in the Russian revolution
without believing in "Socialism."

And so the debates in that Garden of Ideas
were not debates about the possibility, or the
probability, of overturning this old world and
starting a new one. They were debates about
the methods to be adopted in bringing this obvious thing quickly to pass. They were debates
about the relative importance of "personality"

and of "critical thought" in producing this
change, and the relative strength of the different
classes in Russian society, and the rôle which
they might be counted on to play. In particular
they were debates about "Marxism."

And there was a particular reason for this.
It was not Doctor Zif—although the doctor had
read Plechanov's book on Marxian theory and
counted himself a defender of it. Doctor Zif
commanded a very light intellectual artillery, as
he himself has taken pains to demonstrate in a
small book describing his relations with Trotsky.*
No—there was another reason than the erudi-
tion of Doctor Zif why these bold, brilliant

* Doctor Zif is now practicing medicine in New York, a Socialist
of the kind who defended the War-for-Democracy and the pa-
triotism of the Allies. When Trotsky came to New York during
that war—anti-patriot, anti-war, revolutionist to the depth of
his heart—he met Doctor Zif, who he knew had been publishing
a little pro-war paper there in the Russian language. He met
him most cordially; and, wishing to remember the friendly emotions of these earlier days, he invited him to his house. They
talked long and drifted back into the mood of their recollections.
But Trotsky, knowing that Zif could teach him nothing and that
he could convince Zif of nothing, refrained from opening the
political question. It was a characteristically courteous, and a
very friendly, exercise of judgment. But to the doctor's editorial
vanity it seems to have been an unendurable offense, the manifes-
tation of a self-seeking intellectual arrogance which he suddenly
discovered had characterized his friend's activities from the
cradle. Hence this little volume of weak and ludicrous personal
spite. If a worm could snarl it would make a noise like Doctor
Zif's book.

young *Narodniki* could never quite satisfy themselves that they had unhorsed and abolished Marxism. It was the occasional presence at their table, and the vivid image that stayed there after she was gone, of the gentle-eyed, iron-minded sister of the Sokolovskys, Alexandra Lvovna. Alexandra Lvovna was a Marxist—that was what made conversation so uneasy and life a perpetual statement for the defense among these otherwise so confident and unconquerable knights of "the People."

Alexandra Lvovna was older than her brothers. She was six years older than Trotsky, and she had lived through some of the darkest years of the reaction which followed the failure of the Terrorists in Russia. Born in utter poverty and reared by a father who loved the ideal of liberty, she had herself long ago accepted the rebel mood and philosophy of the *Narodniki*. Reading an account of the trial of Vera Zassulitch, remembering the deeds of that time, she could not endure the inaction, the pessimism, the dull color of revolutionary faith among her contemporaries. She was the new generation—she resolved to go again among the people and teach revolt.

It was a resolution which led her first to a

course in midwifery at the University of Odessa, and here she found students who had been at the University of Geneva and had worked with Plechanov and Zassulitch herself and Lenin in the little group called "The Emancipation of Labor," who were sending illegal Marxian literature into Russia. She read the literature and became a resolute adherent of this new and more coldly scientific method for the regeneration of Russia and the world.

She was, to be sure, no profound wizard in the complexities of the science, but she had read enough to make her know that the boys in Svigofsky's garden were as ignorant as they were brilliant and "logical" and was swift to pounce upon anyone who proposed to cool down the lofty emotions with which they were approaching life.

She remembers how they first announced to her the arrival of Leon Bronstein:

"Oh, now you will see! Here is the man who can talk to you! Such logic! *Nobody* can beat him!"

She came to dinner that night expecting some momentous and whiskered professor, who would "inform her of the errors underlying the economic system of Karl Marx," as momentous pro-

fessors have done since the system was invented.
She was utterly amazed when this smooth young
child appeared with the close-cropped black hair
and pale-blue eyes.

Was this the great anti-Marxian debater they
had been telling her about? But he was! From
the first crackle of that voice she felt the force
of the attack, and she defended herself sharply,
ironically. There was hardly a moment of ami-
cability between them. Not only on that occasion, but every time thereafter when they met
some sharp, sarcastic tilt would take place.

"You still think you're a Marxist? I can't
imagine how a young girl so full of life can stand
that dry, narrow, impractical stuff!"

"I can't imagine how a person who thinks he
is logical can be contented with a headful of
vague, idealistic emotions!"

Such is Alexandra Lvovna's memory of their
meetings. And instead of growing more friendly
or more playful as they got better acquainted,
these tilts grew more bitter and frankly hostile
until finally she practically gave up attending
the general meetings of the group.

"For instance, once I insisted on their reading
Plechanov's book, and they threw it on the floor

in rage when they saw his bitter attack on Michaelovsky."

This spirit of fury reached out after her, it seems, even after she had ceased to appear at the garden. There was a *Narodnik* journal in Russia at this time called "The New Word," and this had been subscribed to by the public library of Nikolaev at the request of their group. In the middle of the winter its editorial staff was changed, and its policy became Marxist. As this was the first legal expression of Marxism in the Russian press, the journal was very precious to Alexandra Lvovna. Her emotions were bitter enough when she saw a letter posted in the public library and signed by all her friends in the garden, requesting the directors to cancel the subscription to this journal, which did not "respond to the interests or opinions of the readers."

Svigofsky himself was old enough and wise enough to see the ungraciousness of this act and subsequently crossed out his signature. But it was not Svigofsky, but Bronstein, who had done it, and Bronstein made no attempt at qualification or apology.

Omniscience is of course one of the privileges

of a biographer, and I avail myself of this privilege when I say that it was not only the materialistic interpretation of history against which Trotsky was here rebelling with such ferocity. He has, to be sure, a faculty of burning absorption in problems of mere truth which you and I, chilly Anglo-Saxons, might fail to understand. But he has also a very living heart, and history demands a record of the fact that everybody else in that garden was in love with Alexandra Lvovna. She stood over them as a kind of Madonna, wiser than they, and more tender, and more firm. In this world of halfway things, a shining mind and heroic character have rarely lodged in so gentle and lovely-looking a person.

You will understand a great many peculiar things about the Russian revolution if you understand this quarrel between Trotsky and Alexandra Lvovna. It was the same quarrel exactly, that we saw subsequently between the Socialist-Revolutionaries and the Bolsheviks. It was a quarrel between two ways of viewing human progress so profoundly opposite that no working reconciliation possibly could take place between them. The sincerest Socialist-Revolutionaries are in jail now; they would have jailed the Bolsheviks had they won the power. The difference is that they did not win the power. And they did not win the power because their science was not practical. Let me show you that science at its source:

"The seed of progress," said Peter Lavrov, "is indeed an idea, though not mystically existing in mankind; it is born in the brain of a person; it develops there; afterward it passes out of that brain into the brains of other persons, expanding qualitatively in the increased intellectual and moral worth of these persons, quantitatively in the increase of their number, and it becomes a social force when these persons are conscious of their agreement and decide upon a unanimous activity; it triumphs when these persons, penetrated by it, translate it into social forms."

This viewpoint of Lavrov's was developed by his more shining successor, Michaelovsky, into a whole system of sociology. Michaelovsky made it seem probable—and moreover made it seem scholarly—that the very essence of progress, both in nature's evolution and in human history, was the development of "individuality." And thus those "morally worthy" persons of Lavrov's—the "critical thinkers," the revolutionary intelligentsia—became the goal of progress as well as the power which should carry it forward.

Marx had an exactly opposite idea of the relation of thoughts to a social progress:

"It is not the consciousness of men," he said, "which determines their existence, but, on the contrary, their social existence determines their consciousness. At a certain stage of their development the material forces of production in society come in conflict with the property relations within which they had been at work before. From forms of development of the forces of production these relations turn into their fetters. Then comes the period of social revolution. With the change of the economic foundation the entire immense superstructure is more or less rapidly transformed. In considering such transformations the distinction should always be made between the material transformation of the economic conditions of production, which can be determined with the precision of natural science, and the legal, political, religious, æsthetic or philosophic—in short, ideological—forms in which men become conscious of this conflict and fight it out."

The followers of Lavrov and Michaelovsky believed that Russia's critical thinkers, convinced of the idea of Socialism, would convince the majority of the Russian peasants, or hypnotize them, and that they would establish Socialism without passing through the period of capitalism or awaiting the development of a revolutionary working class. Marx declared that these critical thinkers would have no dynamic effect upon the process, and that even the enormous hordes of the peasants would not play the leading rôle. The relatively tiny number of the workers in the towns alone possessed the force and were in the position to overthrow the old society and create the new.

As capitalism and the factory system inevitably developed, the number of these workers would increase, and their dominating position in Russian life would increase faster than their number. The task of the social idealist therefore was not to carry culture and a Socialist evangel to the peasants, but to teach the industrial workers their revolutionary mission, and organize them for the task. They would have not only to overthrow the czar's government, but to overthrow capitalism as well—for these two tasks were alike, according to Marx, in demanding militant agitation and class war. Culture and the propagation of beautiful social ideals could no more produce Socialism than it could batter down the czar's police.

That was the new doctrine, and the tone of voice in which it spoke. Men like Lavrov and Michaelovsky had proposed a revolutionary social evangel in place of the religious evangels of the past. Marx proposed to replace all evangels with a science of historic engineering. The primary occupation of man, he observed, is earning his living, and the primary motive forces in history are economic. If you wish to mold future history you must calculate these forces as a mechanic calculates the forces of nature, and put yourself in a position to guide them. Instead of an evangelist you must be a technician; instead of a politician, a scientist; instead of a hot and windy preacher, a cool and practical engineer.

This is the doctrine which has given such incredible power to the Bolsheviks in Russia, and which makes the rest of the world look upon them either as saints or supernatural devils, according to the point of view—but never as ordinary, amiable human beings. They are, as a matter of fact, extraordinary. They are "visionaries," using in the interest of their vision that same hard, calculating "business sense" which has always been used by their opponents to make them look ridiculous. They are the "children of light" trying to become as wise in their generation as the children of this world.

But you can see how difficult it was for Trotsky at the age of seventeen, all full of fire and power and the sense of infinite possibilities, to accept this hard discipline of fact from the lips of a lovely young girl. There are two kinds of Marxians. There are those who like Marxism because it gives them an opportunity, as they think, to deny the finer values of life; and they enjoy denying. There are others who like Marxism only as they like facts, and as it is necessary to face facts, in order to go on and build up in concrete reality the finer values of life.

Trotsky's violent resistance to the matter-of-fact interpretation of history, before he had read it or really knew what it is about, was an affirmation of life. It was the expression of a poetic universality and free play of interest over all the interests of man, which in spite of his consecration and superhuman hard work he has never lost. He is as little touched with the disease of revolutionary negativism as any Marxian I have ever met.

Thus his graduation from the high-school at Nikolaev, brilliant and resounding through the town as usual, was not for him a very clear or happy occasion. He felt in his thoughts of himself, even if he did not acknowledge in his "Philosophy of History," the feebleness and futility of a life of lonely propaganda in some peasant village under the surveillance of the czar's police. He had enough "moral worthiness" to send books into the country, but he had not enough scientific folly to go off and bury himself there. In short he did not know what to do with himself. For the first time since he stood up in his crib, swaying and beaming on the whole world, so that people went into the bedroom just to get a laugh out of his blue eyes —for the first time, here at the end of his school year in Nikolaev, his friends describe Trotsky as "gloomy."

He had been sick in the spring, had fainted away as he sometimes does upon a slight provocation, and then gone to bed with influenza. His father, learning of this, had declared a kind of armed truce and come to visit him in the garden. While there he had thrown the entire weight of his character into "counter-revolutionary propaganda." That is, be as revolutionary as you like, but at least have the common sense and decency to urge my son to finish his education!

One of the principal culprits, Galatsky, had failed and moved off to another town, but this resolute father traveled off after him and brought him back to use his influence in behalf of "ordinary common sense." It was a desperate campaign, and if Trotsky's soul was not saved, you need not lay the blame upon this powerful and relentless man.

A friend who stayed often with the Svigofskys, Benjamin Vegman—the editor now of a Communist newspaper in Siberia—has described to me his first vision of Trotsky's father at their garden. Vegman was sleeping on the floor in the living-room, and opened his eyes very early one morning to see this big-whiskered farmer standing over him, aggressive and implacable.

"Hello!" he shouts with a loud voice like a bugle. "You run away from your father too?"

The Russians have a word for stubborn, which means "like the stump of a tree," and that is the word Comrade Vegman used to describe Trotsky's father. We need not wonder, with this giant on one side waging the timeless and irresistible campaign of "common sense," and on the other a beautiful Madonna

offering him the cold and stony-looking doc-
trines of Karl Marx—himself in the middle a
flame of confused radical aspirations—we need
not wonder that Trotsky was "feeling gloomy,"
he whose very genius is to be clear and to be
self-confident.

CHAPTER IV

LOVE AND MARXISM

TROTSKY consented to visit his father "as a guest" during the summer after his graduation. It was the summer of 1896. And during this stormy visit the forces of common sense made their last stand. Trotsky was alone in the field, and his father moved up his reserves in the shape of a prosperous but "liberal" uncle from Odessa. Here was a man who could "sympathize with the aspirations of the working man," but had made his own way, in spite of this sympathy, to the head of a good-sized boiler factory. He was the kind of man who is chosen to "represent the public" on an arbitration board, and his function here seems to have been to "see Leon's point of view" and then lead him by gentle steps back into the path of tradition.

What he did see was that Leon's instinct for revolt against tyranny, born in a baby's protest against this father, could never be conquered or lulled to sleep on the original battlefield.

57

"Get the boy out of the house and stop arguing with him," was his advice. "The more you
insist, the more determined he is."

And so it was arranged between them—at
least Trotsky believes it was arranged—that his
uncle should stumble in upon one of the daily
scenes of battle and offer a practical suggestion
along this line.

Trotsky had just announced "again and for
the last time": "Very well, I will live my own
life!" And he stood there beating off the fiftieth
assault of the old man's intemperate will.

"Is it really necessary," said his uncle, "to
settle this question all at once? Suppose you
come with me to Odessa. My wife will be stay-
ing on here for a while, and we can live together
in my apartment. There is a mathematical faculty at the university, and you can attend some
lectures there—or not, just as you wish—and
take your time making up your mind."

Trotsky accepted this proposition—not without a mental note to the effect that they were
clever, but he could be as clever as they. He
wanted to get out of the house, too. He wanted
to get into the world where he would be free to
consider a problem more engrossing to him than
the problem of his personal career. He might

study mathematics or not; but *what was to be the future course of the Russian revolution?* That was the state of mind in which he left home again, during that August or September, to go and live in Odessa with his uncle.

Trotsky did attend some lectures at the mathematical faculty. His gifts in this direction were enough to tempt him. An engineer in Petrograd, the Technical Director of the Baltic Shipyards, who went to school with Trotsky, described to me the superiority of those gifts. He is a friend of the revolution and proud of his playmate, but he could not keep back a sigh of regret that such an engineer had been lost to the profession. A lightning aptitude for mathematics, a restless constructive imagination, a commanding personality — and then a father with plenty of land, plenty of money, and a monumental ambition to build—it is indeed a miracle that Trotsky did not become an engineer. And in order to understand the unique thing that he did become, it is well to bear in mind this original propensity.

Trotsky even went to call one evening upon the professor of mathematics and open the question of a career in that science for himself. He was cordially welcomed, and the idea enthusiastically endorsed, and he came down the steps thinking:

"How pleasant, and what a pity to waste his time!"

He was wasting his uncle's time, too—talking all evening about Napoleon and about Tolstoi and about Julius Cæsar and about whether the value in his uncle's goods was all created by the workers—a metaphysical question which for some reason people think they have to settle before they can decide whether to revolutionize this world or not. He was supporting here the view of Karl Marx, although perhaps he did not know it, and his uncle was supporting the view of the head of a boiler factory. And behind this view there was also another relative —at least a relative of his uncle—a more cocksure philistine who had amassed a little fortune in the vicinity of Minsk.

"Oh, we all had these ideas in our youth," he said. "Just wait ten years. I'll bet you a kopek that in ten years you will be laughing at all these ideas."

"I don't care to bring my ideas into relation with your kopeks!" Trotsky said.

I wonder how many revolutions will be required before grown-up people learn not to say to children, "I had those same ideas when I was your age."

What made it so shameless for Trotsky to waste his uncle's time in these ideological arguments, was that he was employing his own time in organizing revolutionary "circles" among the workers in his uncle's factory. His uncle knew this, but he never said anything about it. He had taken the job of being a "liberal," and he held to it—until, by the grace of God, his wife came back for the winter, when of course Trotsky moved out.

He went to stay again for a while with the Spencers, earning his living as a teacher, studying a little at the university, playing a good deal and very jovially with his friends and cousins in the evening, but satisfying both the practical and the romantic sides of his nature in the illegal organization of those revolutionary circles.

They were the most amateur organizations you can imagine. Five, seven, or ten persons would come together secretly in somebody's apartment, and they would talk. They would talk about the pressing necessity of overthrowing the czar, establishing a republic, securing freedom of speech, press and assemblage, and calling a strike.

In particular they would talk about the necessity of calling a strike—for some instinct told them that those other necessities, although so pressing, were somewhat old-fashioned. They must call a strike; there was no question about that. But just what to do with the strike after it came, or what relation it might bear to a revolution of the Russian peasantry against the tyranny of the czar and the landlords—upon these points they were not at all clear. They had a "program," however. Somebody showed it a little later to Plechanov in Switzerland, and he laughed.

"They must be children," he said.

They were children, and the most childlike among them in some ways was their leader, around whose radiance they moved as energetically and aimlessly as planets. There never was a more beautiful, there never was a more obviously powerful and startling youth. Trotsky was not yet troubled with any modesty of demeanor. His incomparable ability and his arrant force of character were continually in view.

And so also were his revolutionary intentions. A good policeman would have arrested him on sight. The big shock of uncombed curly black

hair, the shirt unbuttoned at the neck, the suit a
little ostentatiously old and the shoes ostentatiously dusty, but the person delicately clean,
the carriage arrogant, and the tongue as cultivated as it was bold and full of the brag of its
extreme opinions—he was too obviously the rich
man's son going wrong.

And he was intolerant of opposition, too, and
used his terrible charm and facility not only to
attract followers but to beat off rivals. He had
to be the center of every circle and the source
of knowledge, even though he had never read a
revolutionary book and his mind was a mere glit-
tering résumé of radical magazine articles. To
some critical eyes, even within those circles of
admiration, it seemed doubtful if there was anything more stable here than extreme youth and
a romantic taste for outlawry and idealistic
adventure.

Trotsky sacrificed a great deal to that adventure. He abandoned his studies at the university. He gave all the money he could earn
above a simple living. He sat up all night at
those meetings, fervently debating, fervently
teaching what he knew nothing about. In consequence he came so often late to the school
where he earned his living that he was called

before the directors, and a series of conditions were laid down to him, concluding with the suggestion that he should cut his hair and trim himself up like a gentleman. This last condition touched the heart of his "adventure," and he gave up the job.

It was not "serious revolutionary activity," to be sure. It was growth rather than activity. But it was serious enough to attract the attention of the police, or at least so his more cautious comrades assured him. He remains unconvinced of this, but after long disputation, yielding to their urgent advice, he decided to move. On the last boat that sailed down the coast that winter, breaking its way through the December ice, he went back to Nikolaev. He took an *izvostchik* from the port out through the cold to Svigofsky's garden, and he borrowed the money when he got there to pay for it.

Just what Trotsky was going to do here in Nikolaev, aside from earning his meager living as a tutor, was uncertain. He was still valiantly resisting the Marxian theory. He was still defending his "individuality" and the divine importance of "critical thought," and, as a logical although somewhat remote corollary, the divine right of the Russian peasant to conduct the Rus-

sian revolution. But he had not taken the trouble
to look in the eyes of a peasant, and he had in
fact been already at work as an agitator among
the industrial workers.

His practical intuitions were in advance of his
intellectual philosophy. He was a *Narodnik* in
theory and in the moral emotions which controlled his speech, but as a general and a born
man of action he had already placed himself
where the great forces were to be deployed.

Perhaps it was doubt which led him to Nikolaev, a desire to consult again the friends who
had first introduced him to the revolution. Perhaps he had already some dim idea of creating
an organization among the workers in the factories of Nikolaev. Perhaps that passionate
antagonism between him and Alexandra Lvovna
played a part in his going. At any rate the
first notable thing that he did upon his arrival
was not to organize the workers in the factories,
but to organize a new onslaught upon this lonely
and implacable Marxist.

It was one of those elaborate and not usually
very humorous things which we call "practical
jokes." And it was operated in the following
fashion: Not long after Trotsky's arrival in
Nikolaev, and before Alexandra Lvovna had

seen him, Svigofsky arrived at her house to congratulate her.

"Did you know," he said, "that Leon Davidovitch has become a Marxist?"

"Oh, don't tell me that," she replied, laughing. "If you want to fool me tell me something I can believe."

"No, it is true," he answered. "He has been doing a lot of reading in Odessa, and he has turned round completely."

Alexandra Lvovna was suspicious, but as she met other members of the group and they all confirmed this joyful piece of news she began more than half to believe it. She believed it in so far at least as to accept the invitation to a New Year's party at Svigofsky's garden, and that was all that was necessary for the purpose of this historic joke.

She found that the gloominess had all disappeared from Leon Davidovitch's bearing, and the sarcasm too. He was glad and friendly in his greeting, and to her question, "What is this they are saying about you?" he replied, "Yes, yes—absolutely—you don't believe it?"

She did believe it then. But she felt a certain levity in the group, such as usually accompanied their opposition to her more serious nature, and she was not comfortable.

At midnight they all took their seats at the table. A little wine had been provided for this exceptional occasion, and as the clock struck twelve Trotsky arose with his glass and proposed:

"A curse upon all Marxists, and upon those who want to bring dryness and hardness into all the relations of life."

There was more of that speech, but Alexandra Lvovna did not hear it. She pushed back her chair and walked out of the room.

Svigofsky came running after her, begging her pardon and urging her not to be angry.

"You know it was only a little joke!" he pleaded as she was putting on her things.

"I know you would sell your friend and your father for a joke," she said. "There are some things too important to joke about. And you can tell Bronstein that he needn't speak to me again. I don't want to have anything more to do with him."

It was a threat which she made good for several weeks, trying in the meanwhile to gather money to go to St. Petersburg, where she could escape from this magnetic tormentor and work among people who shared her beliefs.

The next thing that Trotsky organized in Nikolaev was a "series of lectures." There is some disagreement about the extent of this series. Some think there was only one lecture, and others think there were two. But at any rate the prospectus was very generous. Each of the dwellers in the garden was to take a certain sphere of "Universal Knowledge" and illuminate it with a discourse, to which the general public would be invited, and which would be followed by an open debate.

Trotsky very generously offered to take as his sphere both "Sociology" and the "Philosophy of History," two subjects about which he knew absolutely nothing at all. He also graciously offered to deliver the first discourse, and he took pains to invite to his discourse the most learned people in the town, including several who did know something about sociology and the philosophy of history.

Now Trotsky had, like all richly intellectual people who can think rapidly, a wonderful gift of bluff. He could catch so quickly the drift of an opponent's thought, with all its mental implications, that it was very difficult to overwhelm him with mere knowledge. He seemed to have the knowledge himself, and a little more too in the same line, before you could get it out of your mouth.

He was not unaware of this gift. Once at a mutiny in Odessa he gave quite an extended report of an article which he had merely heard about; he was persuaded afterward to read the article, and said, "Well, I see he agrees with me!"

What Trotsky was not aware of was the enormous difference between conversation and a lecture. He had no idea what it would be to stand up there all alone in Universal Knowledge with nobody to start him off, nobody to keep him going, nobody to stop him—not a word from anybody but himself.

There is no record of what Trotsky said in this first lecture. No one could possibly have made a record of it. He quoted Gumplowitz and he quoted John Stuart Mill—that much is remembered—and he got himself so terribly wound up in a sliding network of unintelligible big words and receding hopes of ideas that his audience sat there bathed in sympathetic perspiration, wondering if there was any way under the sun they could help him to stop. When he finally did stop and the subject was opened for general debate nobody said a word. Nobody knew what the subject was!

Trotsky walked across the room and threw himself face down in the pillow on the divan. He was soaking with sweat, and his shoulders heaved with shame, and everybody loved him. That was a very important moment in his life. He was born with too much self-confidence, not with too little.

Being delayed in Nikolaev by the lack of funds, Alexandra Lvovna could not very well help falling again into the hands of this indefatigable organizer. This time it was a revolution in the public library that was under consideration. It seems that the directors of the library were elected by the members, who had to pay six rubles each for a membership card; and the mere readers, the general democratic public who came there to use the books, had no voice. The books and magazines were becoming more and more exclusive and aristocratic, and Trotsky decided that nothing but a complete overthrow and seizure of power by the general reader would answer the demands of social justice.

For this purpose it was necessary to arm the

general reader with six rubles, and a meeting must be called to collect these rubles. Well, the best collector in town, as also the best and most intelligent lieutenant engineer in any sort of conspiratorial undertaking, was Alexandra Lvovna. We must hold the meeting at her house!

So Alexandra Lvovna was informed that the public library was about to be overturned and that the conspirators would assemble around her stove on a certain evening.

"I will be very glad," she said earnestly, "to do all that I can."

"It is only fair to tell you," continued the committee, "that Leon Davidovitch is one of us."

"Naturally," she said. "But this I consider a matter of public interest."

And so out of consideration for the public—who were to receive as rude a shock as they ever received in their lives—this private quarrel was again a little prorogued or suspended. To tell the truth Leon Davidovitch himself was not very proud of the New Year's party when he got ahead and looked back at it. He greeted Alexandra Lvovna with an apology, and Marx and Michaelofsky joined hands most cordially in

kicking the "nice people of Nikolaev" out of
control of the public library. A large fund was
collected—more than half of it Trotsky's redoubled earnings as a private tutor.

The annual meeting of the members was
called, and the astonished directors, accustomed
to a routine endorsement from a sleepy half-
dozen, found themselves in the presence of a
large and lively-whispering assembly. They lis-
tened to a proud, gay and presumptuous de-
nunciation from a fiery young man in a blue
workman's blouse and found themselves voted
out without further ceremony. Svigofsky was
elected director of the library, and various more
or less "unsavory" personalities—such as Osipo-
vitch, a Russian novelist who had done his time
in Siberia—were elected to the board of trustees.

The kind of bouquets that grew in this garden
of Svigofsky's was becoming more and more
obvious. It was becoming a matter of public
comment and moreover people were drifting in
there who did not really seem to "belong." An
ignorant, narrow-faced young "engineer" named
Shrenzel arrived in town, a man with an amazing
faculty for revealing his ignorance about everything that interested him. He decided that he

was a disciple of Svigofsky. He sat there listening with stupid intensity like a surprised rat while Trotsky made that midnight speech about Marxism, but he liked it very much and became a great and boresome friend of the orator.

Another indication of their notoriety was the attitude of the two men employed by Svigofsky to work in the garden. One day Trotsky, who was always educating when he was not organizing, put his hand on the shoulder of one of these men, asking whether he knew how to read and write. The man drew back foolishly and made a strange noise as though he were half-witted. Subsequently he recovered his wits and asked Trotsky:

"What is a Terrorist?"

Trotsky explained to him the ideas of the Terrorists—sympathetically, although he himself never believed in their methods.

Another day the younger boy asked Trotsky: "What is a Terrorist?"

And this older man answered explosively, as though he could not contain himself:

"A Terrorist is a brigand!"

A suspicion crossed Trotsky's mind that these men might be spies, but he forgot it again.

It was just at this inauspicious time—in the

spring of 1897—that Trotsky decided to undertake the illegal organization of the workers in the factories of Nikolaev. Gregory, the younger of the Sokolofsky brothers, was the one who proposed it. The fruit trees in Svigofsky's garden were showing the first green-tinted buds, and the wind was coming wet and soft out of the south. The exhilarating miracle of regeneration was all around them while they talked, and they talked with a new sense of the reality of the great event to come.

A new excitement, a new force, was perceptible in the journals that they read. It had been a year of revolutionary awakening, the year of the enormous strikes of the textile workers in St. Petersburg, conducted by the "Union of Struggle," which acknowledged the leadership of Marx and Plechanov. Similar unions had arisen in Kiev, in Moscow, Kharkov, Ekaterinoslav. It was the year when Lenin, at the head of the Petrograd union, first won the confidence of the Russian workers and was shipped off to Siberia by the czar.

It was not a year when a born commander of men, who believed in the liberation of Russia from all her oppressors, could be content to play the game of personality, to organize lectures and intellectual parties, to distribute little innocuous books of culture or even to go off secretly and write a great revolutionary drama, as he and Ilia Sokolovsky had been doing. It was a year for action. All the years thereafter would be—all the minutes of the years—for action. "Faith without works is death"—that was the motto which Trotsky chose for himself in these decisive days.

His good friend Spencer saw him and asked him if it would not be a good idea to finish his education first and then take up the work of agitation.

"There isn't time," he said.

The Marxian propaganda that was finally searching the workers in these days had been born in Russia four years after Trotsky was born. In the year of Trotsky's birth, 1879, Plechanov's philosophic opposition split the old *Narodnik* organization, "Land and Liberty," into two groups—the *Narodnaia Volia,* which consecrated itself to a campaign of individual terrorism, and the *Tchorny Perediel,* which still rested its hopes more or less upon "the People." The Terrorists carried off all the honors of this split, rising thereafter to the height of their power, and becoming upon the assassination of the Czar Alexander in 1881 the most famous revolutionary organization in the world.

But the reaction was swift and terrible. Hanged, exiled and murdered at hard labor by the government of Alexander the Third, the leaders disappeared. The followers lost faith, and Russia entered into one of her blackest periods of political reaction and literary mysticism or despair. It is the period epitomized in Tchekov's writings—a period of the dead hopes of a most heroic movement.

In the mold of these dead hopes the Marxian seed was planted. Plechanov had been driven abroad by the czar's police, and in exile he had studied scientific Socialism. In 1883 he founded in Switzerland a little group called "The Emancipation of Labor," and they began pouring a thin stream of Marxian literature into Russia. In 1885 they issued a "Prospectus of a Program for the Russian Social Democracy," demanding that the workers, winning the sympathy of the poorer peasants, should seize the political power and establish a "temporary rulership of the working class." This still seemed a preposterous suggestion, and might indeed have remained so, had not history taken the pains to prove it.

But factories were building by thousands in Russia in the years that followed; strikes were multiplying; the czar's Cossacks were herding the workers back to their tools, driving in with the thongs of their whips the truths that Plechanov was telling. It was inevitable that the Russian revolution should revive. It was inevitable that Marxians should play in that revival the leading rôle that had been played by the champions of personality and the peasant in the '70's. It was inevitable that a man born in Russia with the birth of the Marxian movement, having the intellectual equipment of an engineer and turning from the mechanical to the social field of engineering, should turn to Marxism.

Trotsky could get no support from Svigofsky in what he had decided to do. Svigofsky had discovered that the elder of the two workmen employed in his garden was to be seen on the other side of the town dressed in the uniform of a policeman decorated for service. He told them that they would succeed in nothing but attracting a *provocateur* and landing themselves in jail. He criticized their opinions and advised against their plans.

Trotsky had only his young friend Sokolofsky with him. He had need of maturity; he had need of a counselor, clear-minded as well as courageous. He knew all along where she was to be found.

"What do you say we go seriously to work," he said, "organizing the men in the factories?"

Alexandra Lvovna agreed. She did not say anything about the change in his theoretical position.

"I thought I would let him find that out for himself," she says.

A long time afterward when they were living together in Siberia she asked him how "a person so sympathetic and sensitive in all the relations of life, could play such a crude trick as he had played on that New Year's day." He told her that he had come back from Odessa with certain doubts in his mind about Marxism, and when he expressed these doubts Svigofsky, instead of criticizing or counseling, had ridiculed him and taunted him with her influence. Then they had cooked up together this heroic last effort to save his soul from the truth.

CHAPTER V

THE WORK AND THE DANGER

TROTSKY was a shining example of that atrocious creature, familiar to all readers of American editorials, the "Outside Agitator." That is to say, he was a man with an extreme social ideal and enough mechanical instinct to know that the only force capable of achieving such an ideal is the organized self-interest of the oppressed classes. He himself possessed no thread of connection with those classes. Sitting there in a garden fragrant with peach blossoms and the memories of high conversation about justice, he was as much puzzled as Plato would have been to find his way to the facts.

Ilia Sokolovsky had once known a worker, a watchman in the public garden, who belonged to a radical religious sect. He might perhaps be radical practically too. Trotsky waited impatiently while Ilia Lvovitch went off in search of this worker. The man had gone away and nobody knew where, but Ilia Sokolovsky brought back the address of some friends of his with whom they might safely open a conversation.

Together they visited these friends, found them in a mood of intelligent revolt against the autocracy, and arrived very quickly at the cause of it—Ivan Andreyevitch Mukhin. Mukhin was a keen-witted mechanic with a sly way of wrinkling up his left eye when he talked, a man of high honesty and authority among the workers. He became the most important member, besides Trotsky and Alexandra Lvovna, of the organization that they formed, and he became one of Trotsky's best friends.

Together they gathered a handful of workmen around a table in the Café Russia, where a mechanical piano kept up enough noise to shield their conversation. They ordered an infinite quantity of tea and began to talk. It was not easy at first—Trotsky felt constrained. But Mukhin knew how to do it. He told them a story like this:

A man pulled a handful of seeds out of his pocket and set one on the table.

"That's the czar," he said.

Around that he placed some other seeds and said:

"Those are his ministers."

Around them some others:

"Those are the generals."

Then came the nobility, the great merchants, and finally the workers and peasants. When it was all arranged another man reached out his hand and mussed up the lot.

"Now tell which one is the czar," he said, "and which the nobility, and which the worker."

Everybody liked that story. It established a community of feeling among them and enabled Trotsky to talk. He was very moderate at first, not saying all that he thought; but the workers themselves were always pushing him forward. Before many evenings they were occupying all the tables in one wing of the restaurant, and one day when Trotsky came early the waiter met him with the words:

"Your folks are not here yet."

That suggested the necessity for a "conspirative apartment"; and this was secured and fitted up by Mukhin himself with a set of electric signals, making it possible in case of alarm to get away by the back door. Here Trotsky drew up a constitution, and this rapidly growing conversational group became the South Russian Workers' Union.

The organization consisted of "circles," which

divided and multiplied very much in the manner
of the cells which compose the tissues of organic
life. The nucleus of the first circle was Trotsky
and Alexandra Lvovna, and its growth was
almost miraculously rapid. When it reached
the prescribed limit of twenty-five members, it
divided into two circles, Trotsky going with one
and Alexandra Lvovna with the other in the
capacity of nucleus—or, as the constitution says,
"organizer."

In the new circle they would each attract to
themselves another person capable of leadership,
so that when another division took place there
would be a nucleus in each circle. In this manner eight or nine circles were formed in the
course of the spring and summer; and in a city
which contained not more than ten thousand
workingmen, over two hundred of them had become dues-paying members of this conspiracy,
all of them knew of it, and the majority read
its proclamations, either with sympathy or excited antagonism.

These proclamations are extremely persuasive
and extremely simple. They speak always about
some concrete thing that just happened in the
factory, the thing that the workers are talking
about as they walk home at night. They speak

in the tone of one who is walking along with them.

"You all know about the recent visit to the shipyards of the captain of the port, Fedotov, and you are all doubtless aroused by the ugly conduct of the rude old man; because a few of the workmen did not bow to the captain they were on the order of 'his excellency' immediately listed for discharge. . . ."

Thus he opens a conversation with the workers in the shipyards.

An engineer in the employ of the bosses has called a meeting to denounce one of his proclamations, and he makes that the occasion of another:

"Neyman climbed up to the top story of the electric-dynamo shop, assembled the workers and made a speech in which there were more lies than words. It was not Neyman but his salary that made the speech. 'You are a mere handful,' cried the salary of Neyman, 'and you dare to revolt against a terrible power!' Ask Neyman, comrades, whether he reads the papers and knows what is happening in this world. Does he know that 46,000 workers in St. Petersburg alone, by means of two strikes, compelled that same terrible power to give them the law of

July 2d concerning the length of the working day? . . . 'You will suffer in prison,' said this engineer, 'and your wives and children will die of hunger and cold.' You understand how he is worried about your welfare? About you and about your wives and children? Answer Neyman, who knows no other joy but a fat meal and a luxurious dwelling, that there is a joy both higher and more glorious—a struggle for the great cause of freedom and justice."

There is no cant in these proclamations, none of that sarcastic propaganda singsong, which destroys the force of so much Socialist writing in America. They speak directly and warmly, and indeed almost with a feminine tenderness, about the problems of the workers and the beautiful future toward which they may move if they will but stand together in courage and friendship. There was still enough of the child in Trotsky to reveal naïvely the quality of the emotion that led him into this life of danger and sacrifice. You can read his heart here in these simple documents, the exquisite little letters printed with his own pen and then mimeographed—patient, artistic, clean, holding out the highest hopes to the lowest class.

"During the past year," he writes on New

Year's day, "many of the workers of Nikolaev joined together in a union and prepared to begin the fight with the bosses; but we shall be able to fight only when you all, comrades, join with us and we unite in one fraternal union. Let us begin a new life with the new year—a life of men battling with their enemies. . . . We do not want to rob or kill; we strive only to make our lives better and better, and to live as men should live.

"Do not believe anyone who says that we are some kind of dangerous persons, some students desiring only to stir up the people. No, comrades, we are workers just like all other workers. Only we want once for all to get out of our poverty and live a human life. We want this not for ourselves only, but for all the workers. . . . Let our first commandment be 'All for one and one for all.' Then we will soon win our right to assemble in the square and openly discuss the workers' cause. Comrades, for our sacred cause we are ready to lay down our lives. . . ."

It is a different Trotsky distributing this serious and humble New Year's resolution throughout the working-class district of Nikolaev, from the brilliant midnight scoffer at Marxism. It has been a long year. Everybody seems to have noticed a change in him. His friends in Odessa, when he came back there to coördinate the work in the two cities, had no more question about the stability of his enthusiasm. If there had been a little of the young rooster in his radicalism before, it was gone now. If they had felt a fear that pride would take the place of purpose—that he would fall, as so many leaders fall, because he could not bear to see other big men beside him—that too was an error.

There will always be something a little arrant about him—always a little of the volcano. That is, he will be a smiling, disciplined, very reasonable and coöperative person; but if something arouses his indignation and he starts to spitting fire, why he will spit fire without any modesty or any regard for the size of the landscape. Trotsky's sense of right and wrong is as arrogant as Christ's, and it is not tempered with a strong love for his enemies. But for those with whom he works and lives, and for the working masses of this world, his will, though so reckless in its force, is altogether a giving and not a grasping one.

As you see in these proclamations, he has completely identified himself, as though he were a poet, with the workingmen for whom he writes. But he is not a poet, and that exercise of imagination must find its sanction in the actions of his life. It will find its sanction in a perfect loyalty.

"He can be very tender and sympathetic," said Alexandra Lvovna, "and he can be very assertive and arrogant; but in one thing he never changes—that is his devotion to the revolution. In all my revolutionary experience I have never met any other person so completely consecrated."

Trotsky had not yet yielded his theory of personality to Marxism; but his personality had yielded to this slender and beautiful Marxist, to her wisdom. He loved her passionately, and he had turned away from every other goal of devotion but her and the revolution. She was altogether different from him, glowing with the seriousness of her faith instead of flashing with its glory, instinctively respecting every other personality, not flooding over with the force of her own. Poised and warm-eyed and practical, gifted with every gift of gentleness, she was a young and well-loved mother to all the workers in their organization. One of them, a very youthful poet named Leikin, wrote verses in her praise:

She is not the goddess nor the saint
Who brought forth Jesus to the earth,
But our organizer is divine,
And she is holy,
Who rescues lost brotherhood
From the ruinous dark.

Hail to her courage!
Hail to her strength!
Hail to her priceless love for us!

It was an organization more like a band of
early Christians perhaps than a modern labor
union. There was more affection and more old-
fashioned goodness in it, and less science and
less business sophistication, than we are accustomed to associate with the colossal idea of organized revolution.

They published in the fall a little magazine
entitled "Our Cause," and this magazine, like
the proclamations, Trotsky himself printed with
his pen. It is a monument of genius and devotion—clean, delicate-lettered, executed with the
patient concentration of a Chinese artist-saint,
and yet in every sentence hot and young and
calling for world-wide action.

Trotsky smiles a little at the "pedantry" with
which he used to perfect this journal, bent over
his table all night long like a diamond cutter

over his jewels. He had spent the day perhaps
running from one end of the town to the other
collecting three rubles to buy the ink and paper.
He had conducted a meeting of his circle in the
evening. The day before he had been on his
weekly trip to Odessa, helping in the organization there, making speeches, establishing a bond
of union between the workers of the two cities.
He had gathered a package of illegal literature,
and with that for a pillow had dropped for his
night's sleep on the third-class deck of the little
steamer traveling back to Nikolaev. On Sunday he had assembled a general meeting of the
union in the woods with speeches, recitations,
greetings brought by a delegate from the workers of Odessa. On Monday he had met the or-
ganizers of the separate circles, explaining the
organization, settling all disputes, arranging
the most minute details of the work. In the
meantime he had written the major part of
his journal, gathering information about the
movement in other cities, in other countries,
making up an economic interpretation of Russian history, composing poetry, writing editorials, manufacturing cartoons by cutting out and
combining the figures from different pictures.
He had earned his vague living in the odd mo-

ments that he could find. And now he would sit up until sunrise night after night, printing this journal with his pen and ink, making each copy clear and exquisite as a prayer-book with his mimeograph machine.

In all this unresting labor in the shadow of danger, nothing was difficult for Trotsky except the "exhibition of his talents." He had not yet learned the three arts of the orator—how to begin, how to keep going and how to stop. The transition from those free-and-easy conversations in the Café Russia to the formal meetings in a conspirative apartment was a thing of dread. And still more the general assemblages in the woods or on the shore of the river, where, like John the Baptist, he would stand in the grass preaching a thing he knew nothing about but felt sure of, to people twice as old as he was. He would read and "interpret" some learned pamphlet that he had got hold of, or he would recite a revolutionary poem or call for their questions and boldly attempt to answer them. What he wanted to do was bolt and run.

One Sunday one of the disciples arrived half full of vodka and wanted to participate in everything that was said. He was led away under the bushes to sleep it off, but he slept only long enough for Trotsky to get a good start and then suddenly poked his head out of the brush and demanded an explanation of Darwin's theory of evolution. He was willing to concede, he said, that men were descended from monkeys, but what he wanted to know, and what he wanted to know before any further discussion, was, what was the first animal born from. He expressed this problem in a language more frank than scientific and almost broke up the meeting, for Trotsky knew practically nothing either about Darwin or about how to get out of an embarrassing situation.

Trotsky knew that he knew nothing. That was what made the situation so embarrassing and so full of infinite promise. There is no rest in Trotsky's sense of himself. The thought of all the things that he does not know is a perpetual exhilarating distress. He has now collected on his desk a little pile of books containing the theories of Einstein and is fretting against the duties that will not let him sit down to master them.* He understands the theory in the same vague way that you and I do, the same way that he understood the science of the revo-

---

* This was written in 1924 when Trotsky was in power.—ED.

lution in Nikolaev. But that is not enough.
Trotsky has a mind of the highest quality—a
mind, that is to say, which perceives precisely
the division between that which it knows and
that which it does not know—and this, combined
with a perfectly dominating desire to excel,
makes him an everlastingly young man, a man
who can not stop growing.

As is well known, the czar had established a
kind of disciplinary free education for young
men of this singular promise, with a revolutionary university in Siberia. And Trotsky was
heading for this course of education with all the
reckless impetuosity of his nature. One day he
came back from his weekly trip to Odessa with
the news that Shrenzel, the stupid little stranger
who hung around the garden, had met him on
the boat, and in the course of their conversation
had asked why there was not a revolutionary
organization among the workers of Nikolaev.

"I wonder if we couldn't use that fellow in
some way," Trotsky said. Alexandra Lvovna
was more prudent, and she disliked Shrenzel.

"He is absolutely without political intelli-
gence," she said, "and we don't know anything
about him. I think you would better leave him
alone."

Trotsky consulted Mukhin, and he too advised him to ignore Shrenzel. But Shrenzel met him again the next week, and his enthusiasm had grown.

"Let's *start* a movement among the workers of Nikolaev!" he said.

Trotsky put him off with some noncommittal suggestion and forgot about him—or tried to. But Shrenzel was always turning up. One day he called at the garden with the news that a worker whom he knew in Kiev had arrived in town, having lost all his documents on the way. There had been a letter of introduction to somebody named "Sophia Michaelovna," but he could not remember the last name.

"Who could that be—Sophia Michaelovna?" said Shrenzel, watching Trotsky's face.

Sophia Michaelovna was the pseudonym of Alexandra Lvovna in their organization.

"I don't know anybody of that name," said Trotsky. "Maybe Alexandra Lvovna does."

She was in the next room, and in order to warn her, he called out: "Do you know anybody of the name of Sophia Michaelovna? Shrenzel wants to know."

Alexandra Lvovna came into the room. "What's her last name?" she said. And as

Shrenzel explained that he did not know, she laughed at the little half bald-headed man whom she detested.

"How do you expect to find a person in a town of this size without her last name?" she asked sharply.

And so Shrenzel went away again without getting what he was after.

In his effort to form bonds of union with the movement in other parts of Russia Trotsky had brought an organizer named Albert Polak from Kiev with a message of greeting from the workers of that city. And in a conversation with Polak he happened to mention this incident.

"Shrenzel!" said Polak. "Why, that's the *provocateur* that disappeared from Kiev! He betrayed one of our comrades to the police!"

Trotsky asked the name of that comrade, and a little later he had Shrenzel in to drink tea with him in Mukhin's apartment. He waited until the man had established himself in his gallantly confidential way beside them at the table and then remarked to Mukhin:

"By the way, did you know that comrade X is coming from Kiev?"

"Comrade X!" Shrenzel exclaimed quickly. "Why, that's one of my best friends!"

"Yes," said Trotsky, still talking to Mukhin, "and do you know what happened to him a little while ago? One of his best friends, one who used to sit often with him at the same table, just as we are siting now"—and he indicated Shrenzel—"denounced him to the police, and they arrested him and ruined his whole life."

Mukhin jumped from his seat.

"Contemptible rascal!" he cried. "I would kill a man like that!"

"Well, there he is!" Trotsky shouted, turning ferociously on the little man, whose lips were white with terror.

Shrenzel testified afterward that Trotsky drew a revolver, and it must have seemed to him like that. He was ordered to get out of the town on pain of death. But it is doubtful if Trotsky knew how to draw a revolver; and it is certain that Shrenzel remained in town and lived to tell the tale in high places.

The police, however, were not depending upon Shrenzel. They had another and more reliable source of information, as Trotsky might have found out one day if he had not been too busy to think. He was busy on his New Year's proclamation. This he was rolling off "the press" in enormous numbers, intending to shower it on Nikolaev like rain. He wanted every worker in town to know about his organization, and in that ambition he was entirely successful.

There were several specially trusted members who helped him in the work of distribution; and the most trusted of all, after Mukhin, was Anani Nesterenko, Alexandra Lvovna's co-worker in circle number two. Nesterenko was very versatile—he could write sublime revolutionary poetry and at the same time keep the accounts accurately.

Trotsky had made an appointment to meet him in a lonely lot on the out-of-town side of the cemetery and deliver a large paper tube full of these proclamations. Nesterenko came a little late, and as Trotsky stood there waiting, a strange man rose out of the dusk by the cemetery wall and walked past him very close, staring at him. In a moment Nesterenko appeared from the same direction. Trotsky asked him who that man was, and he answered with just a noticeable confusion that he did not know.

Trotsky did not give any attention to this incident, but he could hardly fail to realize that the police were actively in search of the source of those proclamations—and not only the police, but a good part of the town besides. All of his prudent friends warned him. Svigofsky had long since abandoned the Utopian garden and hired out to a big landlord in the country; but he came back to his wild brood, attended a meeting and urged them to disband before the whole organization was arrested.

It was clear enough that their work was nearing an end. The ever-bubbling poet, Leikin, meeting an open-minded soldier, had decided that he was worthy to be numbered among the blest and explained to him in full detail just what a proletarian is and what the proletariat intends to do with the world. The soldier went and had a talk with his officer—his mind was open in both directions—and the result was that Leikin was arrested and lodged in the city prison. From Leikin the trail led straight into the heart of their organization. It was only a question of days.

They finally decided to suspend all meetings for a time and disperse. They would allow the trails to cool a little, they thought, and then return and begin again more prudently. But Trotsky knew nothing about prudence. He "dispersed" as far as his father's house, where anybody could find him, and prepared to go to work on the next number of his magazine.

CHAPTER VI

SOLITARY CONFINEMENT

TROTSKY did not take with him his mimeograph machine nor the paper and ink, but arranged to have them brought by a worker whom he promised to meet at the railroad station the next day. He went to the station the next day, and several days after, but the worker did not appear. Trotsky had the material all composed for his journal and was eager as a child with a scrapbook to get to work. Moreover, he was in complete darkness as to what had happened in Nikolaev, and the doubt made him restive.

His father could not help noticing his nervousness, but he said nothing about it. He had been in Nikolaev himself the day after Trotsky left, and they had given him the package, thinking to expedite matters; and he, suspecting its contents, had stowed it under his own bed where it was dark. He watched Trotsky fret with a mixture of distress and satisfaction, until one morning he saw him getting ready to go back to Nikolaev, and then he said:

"What's your hurry? I've got your stuff here. They gave it to me."

Trotsky took it, locked himself up in his room and went to work. He worked all day long and practically all night too. He would come out for a meal once in a while, as grudgingly as a woodchuck in winter, and answer evasively when his parents asked him what he was doing.

It was their turn to be nervous, and they were. They became indeed so deeply distressed that he finally decided to take his machine and his papers and ink and go away. It was the morning of January twenty-seventh, and he saw his father's house then for the last time. They were already building the big, respectable stone mansion, and it stood there in the field without any roof on it.

Trotsky had not been long out of the house when a small army of the czar's police descended upon it and performed what is officially described as a "search." It left the house standing, but the inmost nooks of its walls and ceilings were ransacked, the furniture was thrown about and turned upside down, the upholstery ripped off the chairs, the bedding slashed open, the cupboards were emptied on the floor and the unhappy father and mother left standing amid the ruins, convinced that they had given life to the most dangerous criminal in Russia, and that he would be hanged without judgment if caught. Further than that it accomplished nothing, for Trotsky had all the incriminating material with him under his arm, and he was half a day's journey away. He had gone to Svigofsky's new home, which had been agreed upon by the conspirators as a rendezvous and source of mutual information.

Poor Svigofsky! He never meant to be a revolutionary. He only wanted to be an intelligent man and a carrier of culture to the people. But how could you be intelligent in Russia without getting into trouble? His house stood a little apart from the general farm buildings; it was an ideal place for other people to conspire in. And, besides, the conspirators were his best loved friends. He could hardly have been sorry when he saw Trotsky come trudging through the snow with his big bundle of crime, laughing and full of the plans for his next number. They soon had it untied and all spread out on the tables and chairs and all over the floor, and were working away together like well-entertained children when Alexandra Lvovna's younger sister, Maria, arrived with the news that her brother had just been arrested in Nikolaev and that she had been followed all the way down there by a spy.

"He will be here any minute," she urged, "and you must gather up all these papers and hide them quick."

Trotsky would not take it seriously, and even the prudent Svigofsky insisted on arguing the question before, instead of after, the papers were concealed. Maria Lvovna insisted that she had been followed. She described all the expressive actions with which detectives usually make it a point to reveal their identity, and finally through sheer force of distress prevailed upon them to conceal the papers. They took them out in the cabbage patch and buried them in a deep pit with the cabbages.

Then they came back and continued the discussion. It turned into a discussion as to whether they ought, in view of these arrests, to leave Nikolaev and go and take up their work in some other town where they were not known, or whether that would not merely result in the arrest of the workers they had led, and give color to the propaganda against them as "irresponsible students," "Jews," "outside agitators."

The whole field of revolutionary theory had

to be canvassed in considering this question. Every Russian argument lasts all night. And they were still talking when the lamp grew pale, and Svigofsky remembered that it was time for him to go to his morning chores.

It seemed evident that Maria Lvovna had been mistaken about the detective, and so before going to work Svigofsky dug up Trotsky's portfolio again, and brought it in and set it on the top of a barrel that stood full of water in the entry. He turned around to go out again and met the detective coming in. The man had "planted" them there early in the evening, and then summoned enough help from Nikolaev to surround the house and make sure of their arrest.

He started back with a shock of surprise when he saw Trotsky.

"Oh, that's *you!*" he said, grinning.

His satisfaction was so great that he went rather hastily through the rest of the job, and his "thorough search of the premises" failed to reveal the incriminating portfolio, which sat there all the while in plain sight on the water barrel. Svigofsky, moreover, found an opportunity to whisper to his good-natured housekeeper to be sure to destroy it after they were gone. They rode away in two wagons, Trotsky on a back seat with an enormous gendarme beside him, Svigofsky in front with two gendarmes and Maria Lvovna in the other wagon with the detective.

The old lady was faithful to her charge, but her idea of destruction was a mild one. She took the portfolio out and gently buried it in the snow!

The jail at Nikolaev was not adapted to receive political prisoners, and Trotsky got no better comfort there than if he had been an ordinary criminal—or if he had been a political prisoner in America. For in America we do not recognize a distinction, which seemed obvious to the despots of Russia, between idealistic agitators and common thieves. After fulfilling the formalities at the desk, he was led away through a door of steel bars into a corridor and thence into the nearest room. It was a very big room with one window under the ceiling and no furniture—no bed, table, chair; only a white-brick stove in the wall.

A man was crouched on the floor by the stove in a big overcoat and hat. Trotsky thought at first that this man was a non-political criminal, and for a long time they were both too cautious to speak. Only by way of a long series of intimations did they arrive at an acquaintance. The man was a young revolutionist unknown to Trotsky, a book-binder named Misha Iavitch—"a very dear comrade" as it turned out.

They lived three weeks together in that naked room. They were always cold. The stove was half-heated, and there was a six-inch grating in the door, where the frost blew in from a corridor separated only by an iron lattice from the open air. Not once all day did they take off their rubbers or their overcoats or hats. At night straw mattresses were brought in, and they lay down on them, close to the stove and close to each other, covered with everything they had.

At six o'clock in the morning they were roused by the guards, and as they had no will to move the mattresses were yanked from under them. They dressed hastily and then drowsed again for two hours, sitting on the floor with their backs to the stove. Hot water and prison food were brought to them by "trusties," and through these they managed to establish a communication with the other rooms.

They had no pencils, but would write by pricking holes with a pin under the letters in old scraps of newspaper. In this way Trotsky learned of the arrest of all the leading members of his organization, twenty-eight of them, including Alexandra Lvovna.

The news of Trotsky's arrest had reached Alexandra Lvovna in Ekaterinoslav, where she had withdrawn when the organization dispersed. She learned also of the failure of the detective to find the incriminating evidence; and, thinking that they might all be examined and released more quickly if she were present, she came back purposely into the zone of danger. It was a naïve calculation, and characteristic of this most youthful and imprudent conspiracy. She was arrested in the railroad station upon her arrival.

They were in jail ten months before there was any hint of an examination. And during those ten months the snow had time to melt around that eloquent portfolio, and the summer grass to grow up and conceal it; the grass had time to grow too high and be cut down by Svigofsky's diligent successor; and the children of the landlord, playing there, found the portfolio and carried it to their father. He, being loyal to the czar, or—what is the same thing—prudent of his own skin, turned it over in due course to the police. That sealed the fate of the South Russian Workers' Union.

There were six "intellectuals" properly so-called among those arrested. The remaining twenty-two were manual workers—steam-fitters, cutters, joiners, boiler-makers, blacksmiths, book-binders, a seamstress and a soldier. In this small city which had never heard of a labor union, Leon Trotsky, only eighteen years old, had organized in nine months over two hundred of the workers of these essential industries in a criminal conspiracy on a programme calling for the overthrow of the existing government and the expropriation of the capitalist class. You can imagine the confidence that he inspires, the restless and compelling force of his character. You can understand how the Red Army rose up out of the wreckage of a nation and fought off the world.

It would have been a good idea to keep this young man warming his back against a cold stove all the rest of his life. And you wonder why it was not done. Why do government officials who have no fundamental regard for their own laws, have any regard for them at all?

After three cold weeks with his young comrade in the jail at Nikolaev, Trotsky was led out alone one day, placed in a mail-wagon with two gendarmes and driven thirty-five miles through the country. He found himself at nightfall in the city of Kherson, where the jail was not so crowded perhaps—or where his friends would not be able to guess his whereabouts and communicate with him.

Trotsky lived in absolute solitary confinement in a small cell in this jail for about two months and a half. It was warmer here, but the warmth was due only to the absence of openings, and the air was correspondingly foul. Trotsky had no clean linen and no hope of receiving any; and there was no soap, and he found himself covered with lice. He had no book, no paper, ink, pencil. The fight with lice occupied a considerable part of his time, and he would keep walking from one corner of his cell to the other, counting his steps or making up verses and committing them to memory. The loneliness, the inactivity, the loss of his friends, the inability to look forward to anything, and worst of all perhaps the nervousness caused in him by the filth of his body, would bring waves of anguish through his thoughts.

But his will was strung tight. There was no relaxation of its mettle. "For our sacred cause we are ready to lay down our lives."

A wonderful generation of men and women

was born to fulfill this revolution in **Russia.**
You may be traveling in any remote part of
that country, and you will see some quiet, strong,
exquisite face in your omnibus or your railroad
car—a middle-aged man with white, philosophic
forehead and soft brown beard, or an elderly
woman with sharply arching eyebrows and a
stern motherliness about her mouth, or perhaps
a middle-aged man, or a younger woman who is
still sensuously beautiful, but carries herself as
though she had walked up to a cannon—you will
inquire, and you will find out that they are the
"old party workers." Reared in the tradition
of the Terrorist movement, a stern and sublime
heritage of martyr-faith, taught in infancy to
love mankind, and to think without sentimen-
tality, and to be masters of themselves, and to
admit death into their company, they learned in
youth a new thing—to think practically; and
they were tempered in the fires of jail and exile.
They became almost a noble order, a selected
stock of men and women who could be relied
upon to be heroic, like a Knight of the Round
Table or the Samurai, but with the patents of
their nobility in the future, not the past.

Trotsky belonged to this noble order, and his
years in jail were but a part of the appropriate

experience. They made him a member of the oppressed classes whose cause he had championed. He would not be an "outside agitator" any longer. There would not be an excess of sympathy in his mood of revolt. He could hate the tyrant on his own account, and fight for his own right of liberty.

The verses which Trotsky made up show how revolutionary his mind was in this torture of solitude, and how unpoetic. He made up verses that he thought might help to overthrow the czar. If he had been a poet he would have overthrown the czar in verses. Only two of these verses survive. One of them is a soap-box ballad-lecture, written to the music of the "Komarinskaia." The other is called "My Little Machine" and may be described as the revised, or Marxian, version of a revolutionary folk-song belonging to the boatman of the Volga. In that song the Russian peasant tells the virtues of his "little oak club." He turns to it in all the major crises of life, and finally brings it down on the head of the czar:

> Oh, Dubínushka, heave-ho!
> Oh, the little green one
> Lifts of itself.
> Give her a twitch and—ho!

That is a free translation of the chorus, and Trotsky's revised version sings:

> Oh, Machínushka, lightly!
> Oh, the little steel one
> Runs of itself.
> Oil her, and let her go!

"My verses are very bad," Trotsky says. And his critical judgment, I will add, is very good. His poem is printed in the Bolshevik song books —but this for pedagogical, I imagine, rather than lyrical purposes. "You may *sing* about the peasant and his little oak club," says the Executive Committee; "but when you get through singing, read this, and don't forget that we are Marxian and by no means Socialist-Revolutionaries."

One morning toward the end of his three months in Kherson Trotsky's guard arrived, carrying a pillow and a blanket, tea, sugar and some good things to eat, and wearing an expression of Christian benevolence with a market value of ten gold rubles. These had been paid outside the prison walls by Trotsky's mother. With those elementary properties he was able to institute one or two little infinitesimal habits of life that gave some relief to the bare sitting and

standing.   And this kind of relief continued
throughout the two years of his imprisonment.

About the first of May, three months after his
arrest, Trotsky was again led forth between two
policemen and loaded into a patrol wagon.   And
this time he found himself, upon dismounting, in
his familiar sleeping-quarters on the deck of the
night boat to Odessa.   He was taken to the big
modern prison in that city, and there he spent
two very important years of his life.

I asked him in a letter to amplify some of the
things that he told me about those years, and
his answer, hastily dictated, is better than my
story:

You ask me about the Odessa prison.   It was radi-
cally different from the prisons of Nikolaev and Kherson.   Those were old provincial prisons adapted chiefly
for non-political criminals.   The Odessa prison represented, as you might say, the last word in American
technique.   It is a solitary-confinement prison with
four wings, containing several hundreds of single cells.
Each wing has four stories, and along each story runs
a metal gallery, and those galleries are joined together
by a system of metal stairways.   Brick and metal,
metal and brick.

Steps, blows, movements clearly resound throughout
the whole building.   The beds attached to the walls
fold up in the daytime, and are let down at night.

You can hear distinctly when your neighbor closes up or lets down his bed. The prison guards signal to each other by striking with metal keys on the metal rails of the galleries. That sound you hear almost continually throughout the day. Steps on the metal galleries you hear also distinctly, as well as steps next door to you, and under you, and over you. You are surrounded by an uninterrupted noise and clangor of brick, cement and metal. And all the time you are absolutely isolated.

In spring the windows were opened, and the convicts, standing on their tables, would call across to each other. That was of course strictly forbidden, and at times the administration actually achieved "order." But there were periods of weakening, when conversations went at full swing.

I was brought to the Odessa prison in May, and when I first showed my head at the window they named me "May." (We each had our conventional prison designation, so that the guards, listening in on our conversations from the court, could not guess who was speaking with whom.) I, however, participated little in the conversations, since these shouts through a window give little and at the same time make you very nervous.

The politicals occupied one of the wings and were supervised not by a guard but a member of the police force. An old non-commissioned police officer, Usov, was our almost unlimited ruler. He was an intelligent and crafty man, poised, not lacking in good-will, and inclined to a bribe. His assistant was Miklin—a neurotic with a woman's face, eternally singing sacred hymns through his nose, pious to hysteria.

Usov brought me books from the prison library. Sometimes they would be works of polite literature, oftener historical journals—the "Historic Messenger," and especially in great quantities the "Orthodox Review" and the "Pilgrim." After three months without a single printed line I threw myself ferociously upon books. Theological journals I read weekly with the same ardor as the "Historic Messenger" or the works of Korolenko. The polemics of the learned orthodox writers against Voltaire, Kant and Darwin led me into a world of theological thoughts, which I had never touched before, and I had never even distantly imagined in what fantastic, pedantic, droll forms these thoughts pour out.

Those books contained an odd history of the prison, for the convicts have a habit of relating there, by means of little dots under the letters, the facts about themselves—who they are, when arrested, and for what cause. A considerable time must have passed before I began to receive books from the outside. At any rate I managed to read the files of the "Orthodox Review" for a long series of years.

I had known the prison tapping alphabet before my arrest, but none of my neighbors knew it. I was not especially sorry, for books swallowed me completely. After some weeks of my stay in the Odessa prison my neighbor on the right began insistently tapping to me. The tap was not in the prison alphabet, but monotonous, even unintelligible and tiresome. I judged that some illiterate convict was tapping on the wall from sadness, and did not answer. On the next day and the day after it continued. Then it came into my head that my neighbor did not know the prison alphabet, and was tapping each letter according to its place in the alphabet. As an experiment I cried out. My neighbor tapped with redoubled energy. The first letter was S—nineteen blows on the wall. I thought to myself, half-joking:

"What if it should be Sokolofsky!"

The second was O, the third K, and so on. It was Sokolofsky! I soon taught him a better method of tapping, and he told me that he had been about two months in Kherson, whence he had been transferred like me to Odessa.

After about two weeks or more we found out that there was a secret communication between our rooms. The prison toilet had a drain which entered the wall from two sides—that is, from the two neighboring rooms it went into the same wall, and more than that into the same ventilator shaft. The lower part of that ventilator shaft was walled with only one brick. The convicts in almost all the cells had knocked out that brick and established a connection with one of the neighboring rooms.

Sokolofsky and I could even see each other, could pass notes, shake hands and exchange unbound books; for this it was only necessary to remove the table and toilet from the wall.

Usov noticed our illegal communication, but shut his eyes to it. After a month or two some new police officer took charge of us, and then I was moved to another cell.

By that time I was already receiving books from the outside. I had the New Testament in five languages (Russian, German, English, French, Italian) for the study of foreign languages. I studied the Italian language with special diligence at that period, learning Italian poetry by heart. The New Testament I learned admirably, could recite accurately the separate chapters and separate verses in them.

During my promenade I used to tease the pious officer Miklin, demonstrating to him that he played the same rôle toward us as the Roman soldiers toward the Christian saints. In answer he informed me that the heretic, Arius, had exploded alive because he called the Mother of God simply the Mother of Christ—and Miklin left me to conclude what fate awaited me in view of my arbitrary operations upon the text of the Holy Scripture.

The inquiry into the Nikolaev affair took place in the prison ten or eleven months after I was arrested. The Nikolaev police lieutenant, Dremliuga, put the questions. He had in his hands at that time all the material which I left in the country at Svigofsky's . . . and it was amply sufficient to convict us. I presented a written explanation with the purpose of proving that Svigofsky had no connection with the affair. At that period it was not yet accepted as a general rule in the ranks of the revolution to abstain from all testimony. Dremliuga questioned me not more than twice.

After my removal to the new cell I found myself next door to Zif. He too was a welcome neighbor, although less interesting than Sokolofsky, with whom I was bound by common literary interests.

I read in prison: Darwin, a complete collection of the works of Michaelovsky, Plechanov—"Toward the Development of the Monistic View of History"; Antonio Labriola on Historic Materialism, and many books on the history of freemasonry, and in connection with these upon the history of guilds in the Middle Ages and social conditions in the seventeenth and eighteenth centuries.

From the first day that I received paper and ink I began to formulate for myself the theory of historic materialism upon the foundation of what materials I had at my disposal.

When it seemed to me that I had made the matter clear to myself in the abstract, I decided to make an experiment in the application of the method to some more or less complicated ideological question. The choice, rather accidentally, fell upon freemasonry; I hit upon that subject while reading a historical work by Pipin—the title of the book I have forgotten. Since it was necessary to return the books in order to have the right to receive new ones, I made enormous summaries in my note-book, sometimes running to ten pages in the most minute handwriting. By the end of my stay in the Odessa prison I had filled with these summaries a fat note-book of several hundred pages. This note-book, along with all my work on freemasonry, got lost later in Switzerland.

I remember telling you that in the first days of my confinement in prison I acknowledged to myself that I had become a Marxist. Darwin destroyed the last of my ideological prejudices. Marx himself I could not secure in the prison. Beltov and Labriola I received later. In the essence of the matter I was already a Marxist outside, but through obstinacy I still defended, against the Marxian epidemic that was spreading among the intelligentsia, my "individuality," a sufficiently ignorant one.

I communicated the news of my conversion to Svigofsky, being confident that he had gone through a similar process. To my enormous surprise he received my announcement very coldly, and had not the slightest inclination toward Marxism. After that Sokolofsky declared himself a Marxist, as I had. Zif already counted himself a Marxist before the imprisonment.

In the Odessa prison I felt something like hard scientific ground under my feet. Facts began to establish themselves in a certain system. The idea of evolution and determinism—that is, the idea of a gradual development conditioned by the character of the material world—took possession of me completely.

Darwin stood for me like a mighty doorkeeper at the entrance to the temple of the universe. I was intoxicated with his minute, precise, conscientious, and at the same time powerful, thought. I was the more astonished when I read in one of the books of Darwin, his autobiography, I think, that he had preserved his belief in God. I absolutely declined to understand how a theory of the origin of species by way of natural and sexual selection, and a belief in God, could find room in one and the same head.

There, that is the most that I can tell you about my stay in the Odessa prison.

Trotsky's crime was sufficient, if he were formally tried and condemned in court, to earn him twenty years at hard labor in the mines. But the publicity of formal trials was not always convenient to the czar's government. In wholesale quantities political rebels were simply shipped off to the northern villages of Siberia by administrative order, and there set at liberty under police surveillance. As there was but one way out of these villages, along the river valley, they had the character of stockades or big prison-yards. Trotsky and his principal co-workers were sentenced to four years in one of these stockades.

It was a late autumn of 1899, almost two years after his arrest, when Trotsky was finally led out of his solitary cell and down into the office of the prison, where he joined his old friends of the garden. Alexandra Lvovna was there, and her sister and brothers, and Svigofsky, and Zif, and Mukhin—all the best friends that he had in the world—and they were shipped away together in a comparatively jolly company.

They spent the winter in the "transfer prison" in Moscow, and there Trotsky and Alexandra Lvovna were married. That marriage had been planned long before in the prison in Odessa, but Trotsky's father had stopped it by means of a telegram to the Minister of Justice at Petrograd. He put all the blame now upon Alexandra Lvovna, and believed that by stopping this marriage he might still rescue his son and get him to build sugar-mills on the Bronstein estate. I doubt if he ever fully relinquished that purpose until a detachment of his son's army marched in and took the estate away from him. But here in Moscow they were beyond his observation, and their union was legally sealed and sanctified by a rabbi-chaplain with an old ring borrowed from one of the prison guards. This was not because Trotsky and Alexandra Lvovna needed the blessings of a church or of the laws upon their love. It was in order that, as man and wife, they might be exiled to the same village. That was the "marriage problem" for Russian revolutionists. They were often married when they were not lovers, as well as when they were.

Trotsky and I visited together the prison in Moscow where he was confined so many years ago. He showed me the dim semi-circular cement room in the Pugatchevsky Tower where he and his friends slept on board bunks radiating from the curved wall. He showed me the little courtyard where they played *lapta,* a kind of Russian cricket, and where one day Trotsky got thrown on his back and dragged out to the lock-up by the prison guards. The superintendent in those days was a big German-Russian bureaucrat, a pompous and brass-buttoned official, who gave orders that when he appeared in the court the prisoners should remove their hats. He appeared in the middle of a game and Trotsky, who was standing nearest to the gate he came through, paid no attention to him at all. He advanced with a loud roar, commanding Trotsky to take off his hat.

"Don't yell at me—I'm not your soldier!" Trotsky said.

The man called for the alarm whistle, and amid that appalling din ten or twelve guards rushed in, leaped upon Trotsky and dragged him off to another tower to live on bread and water for his sins. But Trotsky's sins are always organized. Every one of the political prisoners followed his example—they all had to be dragged off in the same way—and the job of punishment was too heavy. It resolved itself into a general change of residence, which was not unwelcome to them; for the new cells, although smaller, were not so crowded, and the question of saluting their pompous ruler was allowed to lapse.

Trotsky's home-coming to this prison after twenty-two years was a simple one. The power has changed hands, but the pomp has disappeared. There are no brass buttons in Russia. As the terrible gates swing open at the approach of Trotsky's car a good-natured, fat-faced, teacher-like character in a workman's coat runs forward, jumps on the running-board and shakes hands as we drive in. He is excited by Trotsky's visit to his prison—as excited as though Trotsky were the Czar of Russia—but his excitement shows itself in an amiable, comradely eagerness rather than in any access of dignity. Bolshevik prisons are informal and easy-going in comparison with American prisons. They are a little bit more like schools, and it is easier to graduate from them. They make you feel glad that the power has changed hands.

It was spring again before Trotsky and his companions started eastward from Moscow, and they were on the road all summer, stopping for long months in the prisons of Irkutsk and Alexandrovsk. At the end of August, 1900, he and Alexandra Lvovna were placed on a big river barge with a crowd of criminal prisoners and *skaptzi*—a sect of fanatic men and women who castrate themselves in order to become altogether hideous and egotistical for the glory of God—and with this company they floated down the river Lena toward their home under the Arctic Circle.

CHAPTER VII

WE have an idea that to be "sent to Siberia" is the last extreme of human torture, but our idea is based upon the experience of hard-labor convicts, not of administrative exiles. Trotsky's life in that chilly village to which he was condemned as an enemy of the state was far richer than that of most of the inhabitants condemned there by the accident of their birth. It was a simple and romantically tranquil life, the kind you think of and wish, for a moment, you might live when you see out of the car window some picturesque little thatched cabin with roses or a snowdrift at the window. He was a generous and laughter-loving husband and companion, the affectionate father of two baby daughters, skillful with a broom, a firm-handed dish-washer, an early wood-chopper, and expert in the art of keeping the cook sober until after dinner-time. The cook was a fellow exile, Miksha, a political-minded Polish shoemaker in real life, but in this drama of the revolution a traveler lost in the arctic snow with nothing left about him but charming good humor and a terrible thirst.

Ust-Kut was the name of the village to which Trotsky and Alexandra Lvovna were exiled; but after a year there they secured permission to move southward to Nizhnie-Ilinsk, where a physician was available. And then after six months they moved again to the larger town of Verkholensk. But in all these places they lived the same tranquil life, the life of a Siberian peasant family, softened by the receipt of nineteen rubles a month from the government, enriched by the study of science and the world's literature and enlivened by the periodic arrival of mail and newspapers and the occasional passage of comrades and fellow-rebels, traveling north with resignation or traveling south with eagerness.

Among these passers-by Trotsky remembers seeing for the first time A. M. Uritsky, later the President of the Petrograd Soviet, who was murdered in the counter-revolution in 1918— "Uritsky with his unchanging, tranquil, kindly smile." Here too he first saw Dzerzhinsky, the man who was chosen because of the terrible strength and purity of his motives to be the head

of the Extraordinary Revolutionary Committee
—the Saint of Terror.

"At night around the fire," said Trotsky, "he
read us his poem in the Polish language.   I
cannot remember the poem, but the face of that
youth, so extraordinarily beautiful in its spirit-
uality against a background of firelight, is still
clear in my memory."

These were beautiful moments.   But a more
reliable excitement was the arrival of a three-
horse sleigh which brought mail and newspapers
from the capital.   It came once or twice a week
in good weather; when roads were bad, once a
month, or once every month and a half.   And
the exiles dived into these newspapers like rab-
bits into a lettuce-patch, devouring them line by
line in greedy silence.   And if the sleigh did
not arrive when it was due, or if it arrived too
late in the evening for immediate distribution,
then they trudged home and sat round the table,
solemn and angry.

One evening when everybody else had given
up and gone to bed Trotsky put on his big boots
and overcoat and walked back to the post-office
for a last look.   The sleigh was there—and
moreover when he entered the door he passed
the police captain coming out with a letter in

his hand. The letter crept under his uniform as he went by; but Trotsky saw it and rushed on up to the door he had come out of and demanded his mail. The postmaster looked him over and refused.

"It's too late," he said.

Trotsky is one of those unreasonable beings who never give up the idea that things are supposed to be just. He raised a storm around that post-office more like a nobleman than a convict, denouncing the illegality of the discrimination, calling all Russian law and history to witness against it, and so badly frightening the obdurate postmaster that he went into court subsequently and accused Trotsky of "obstructing him in the fulfillment of his official duties." The court found Trotsky guilty and fined him three rubles, but he got away from Siberia leaving it unpaid—"among my many other debts," as he says, to "czarism."

Trotsky's chief debt to czarism at this period of his life is the perfection of his literary style. He just needed to be snowed up in a little Siberian village with nothing but paper and ink to entertain him. He had the one indispensable gift—what the books of rhetoric call "sincerity," although the sincerest rarely possess it—the ability to be oneself with a pen.

But an artist has to train himself up to the level of himself. And that is what Trotsky did here in these idle years at the expense of the imperial government. He had not been three weeks in Ust-Kut before he began trying to make literature out of the life there. He sent his first effort to a newspaper in Irkutsk called the "Eastern Review," and it was printed. It looked beautiful!

Trotsky was filled with excitement, and plunged headlong into the life of a literary artist. He read and studied the literature of the whole world, tasting its qualities in five different languages, copying out extracts, estimating, molding his own style as he wished to have it. All night long he would sit up at his table, writing, rewriting, rejecting, writing again, until he would have something in his hand at dawn that he could weigh and believe in.

He was not allured into thinking of himself as a great creative writer. He had perhaps too generous a gift of literary appreciation for that. He loved his heroes too well—loved Gogol too well. He thought of himself as a revolutionary journalist, as one whose art would be pamphleteering, and his style a fighting style. But he was doing something, and he had to do it well, and so his penal years in Siberia became years of the most refined and fervent growth.

You would have a hard time finding in Trotsky's "column" in the "Eastern Review" the fierce and rabid trouble-hunter that you perhaps believe him to be. What you find is a genial and humane essayist of the smilingly discursive type of Charles Lamb—or perhaps it would be better to say of the type of Heywood Broun. For Trotsky seems to have been one of the founders of that modern art of being a complete human being upon the editorial page of a newspaper.

"The reader will not complain against me," he says, "if in our future conversations I mix together in one all journalistic-literary forms and kinds; if the general 'guiding thought' subsisting ordinarily under control of the watchful eye of the editorial writer is illustrated with private facts, the publication of which constitutes the task of the correspondent; if personal observations upon the life of this or that rural corner are brought into relation with the authoritative printed opinions."

After some little explanation in this kind Trotsky proceeds to establish himself in that newspaper as the friend of its readers. He is a literary critic, a dramatic critic—if one can dramatically criticize a lantern-show in the town hall—a philosopher of domestic relations, of education, of art, poetry, feminism, morals and international politics—kindly, keen and humorous and not unpoetic, loving justice, loving truth, loving all kinds of excellence and not finding any topic either too momentous or too trivial for his acute judicial attention.

He tells you about the perplexities of a neighbor whose child got bit by a mad dog, and he tells you why Nietzsche found it necessary to transvaluate values. He commiserates the fate of lunatics in the country, and adds that doctors themselves are not much better off for company; suggests a county medical congress and enumerates its uses. He describes with boisterous irony a stereopticon lecture on the career of a great Russian general, meditates upon the uses of history and suggests that it would go better if they would raise the screen.

He surveys the feminist movement with sympathy, declares that its goal is to "break the icy rind of dull reserve surrounding women of the

middle class and the timid distrust even of the
most 'emancipated' male," and shows that he
himself is only an emancipated male by declar-
ing that it has already achieved that goal. He
explains the failings of Gogol as a moral philosopher and pays an infinitely loving tribute to
his truth-telling art. He finds Max Nordau
"more broad-talking than deep, minutely envi-
ous and not stingy with energetic phrases." And
Nietzsche, he says, is too cloudy and contradic-
tory to be explained except by examining the
social soil that produced him; he examines that
soil and finds it "rotten, malignant and infected."

Gorky he sets aside somewhat reluctantly—
just as Gorky has now set himself aside—as a
rebel and not a revolutionist. Gorky represents
the revolt against society—says Trotsky in 1900
—not the revolt of the proletariat within it. His
characters are down, not because they fell van-
quished in the contemporary social struggle, but
because they held themselves superior to all contemporary society and withdrew from it. They
are in fact "supermen," and Gorky is akin to
Nietzsche in his irrelevance to the social problem.

That perception—or that prophecy—will show
to what extent Trotsky had mastered here at
the age of twenty-two the intellectual and emo-

tional technique of the coming revolution. He had found his equilibrium. You sometimes feel in reading these essays that they are a little too literary, a little bit "high-brow." But you never feel any of the overstrain of a youth who is trying to convince himself of something, or to vanquish his opponents with an inadequate weapon. He is very confident of his opinions— as behooves those who are learning to write— but he shows a mature and surprisingly gentle explicitness in expressing them.

He is cruel to those who are without mercy, and without mercy to those who are cynical. But the weak, the sentimental, the professorial, the trivial, he is content to understand. And he understands without dogma. He does not feel compelled, as do so many believers in a cause, to deny in the interest of his belief the fundamental variety of life's problems. Repressed by the censor and robbed of the possibility to write revolution, he is able to write of other things with force and enthusiasm.

"Reader," he cries in one place, "we must raise the banner of revolt!" But it is only the continual appearance of abominable translations that evokes this note of violence.

It is one of the strange dispensations of our

pecuniary gods that so long as the editorial
column expresses their interest with orthodox
stupidity the book-reviews may be slightly intelligent. And Trotsky, like many another obscure
lover of truth, availed himself of this circum-
stance in order to "put across" occasionally a
fundamental political idea. His ideas were
popular, and he was soon recognized and re-
warded by the "Eastern Review" with three
kopeks a line—a sum which made life a little
easier on the banks of the Lena than the imperial government had ever intended it to be. He
received, moreover, at the expense of his newspaper, contemporary journals and reviews from
St. Petersburg, and was thus able to keep in
lively touch with the events of the world.

In 1902 he had a meeting with his editor and
received an offer of sixty rubles a month as a
regular contributor of *feuilletons*. He came
back to Verkholensk amused and triumphant
and prepared to enjoy to the full his extraordinary genius for being swindled by kind friends.
But the joy was short. He had that great fortune only long enough to start spending it. In
the place of his first pay-envelope came the news
that the imperial censor at St. Petersburg had
written to the editor stating that the contribu-

tions signed by "Antid-Otto" * would no longer be received for consideration. The editor was regretfully compelled to withdraw his offer, and Trotsky's first literary career came to an end.

In one of his contributions he described the domestic life which he encountered in his first home in Siberia. It will give you an impression of his style as a novice in literature.

FROM A RURAL DIARY

Province   of   Irkutsk;
Department of Polynsk;
Village   Urgutsk.
Male population .. 279
Female population. 290
Domiciles 91

Such is the location of our village, and its "poll capacity" as our assistant town-clerk expresses it on wooden boards attached to posts at the two ends of the town.

Urgutsk is to a certain degree an administrative center, and thus the "ruling classes" are fairly well represented—the justice of the peace, a college man, still young, with very slender mustaches and perfumed pocket-handkerchief; the commissioner of agriculture; the police captain; the revenue officer, a small, fine-

---

* The Italian word for *antidote*, a name which Trotsky found by opening at random his Italian dictionary.

edged man of the type that is portrayed on boxes of shoe-polish. . . .

Upon the spiritual side: Our pastor, a bustling Siberian priest who devotes much of his energy to horse-trading and other forms of commerce and is in general addicted to this world and its vanities; the deacon, who teaches the children in our parochial school and expresses himself concerning our local correspondent—alas, we have one—as follows: "And that pest has been scribbling again!" finally the psalm-reader, a sentimental and given to telling his lady friends how he "hit it up with the boys" on the road from Chiliabinsk: "Didn't we hit it up though!" he says, smacking his lips. "Simply delightful! I got so gay that— But you must pardon my frankness!"

In the absence of the priest this psalm-reader once summoned "the world" with the sound of the church bell in order to raffle off his share of the clerical meadow-grass.

The son-in-law and chief assistant of the county clerk, who formerly fulfilled two positions, and that of psalm-reader among them, reported this incident at the county seat (Deacon asserts that "the pest" reported it) and the ecclesiastical superintendent issued an ungracious paper: "In consideration of this misapplication of the sacred reverberations——"

I live with a well-to-do *moujik* who, they say, made his money dishonestly. I do not know whether that is true or not, but I like him better than the other *moujiks* of Urgutsk. He is not so greedy, is unusually hospitable, carries himself with a certain dignity and is no fool. His wife is of like character. But they both drink to a degree unusual even in drunken Siberia.

"Everybody is at work in the harvest," says the little old lady—something in the nature of a twice-removed aunt, who is living out her life with our landlord—"but our folks are drinking and cannot stop."

The old lady is already over eighty, but exactly how much over eighty she does not know; maybe it is five, maybe it is fifteen, years. She is small-sized, all shriveled up, with fingers half-clenched over a cane, a real grandmother of the kind that you see in pictures. Grandmother fully retains her sound sense, however, and does not keep telling us about "the good old days."

"In our time it was bad—terrible!" she says, looking past you and nodding her wrinkled head. "Look at them! Look at these hands, what they are from work! For fifteen kopeks a day what didn't I do?—Terrible! Now it is better; life is easier. A little free money in the house. But they drink and drink. They ought to hold each other back. But they've lost the way; they drink all the time. Terrible!"

And then, leaning toward you, she continues in a kind of aggrieved whisper:

"And it's all *her* fault! He drinks and sleeps it off, but he finds her drunk—nothing is warm in the house, nothing is cooked, nothing swept—he gets drunk again. Then she comes to, and he is sprawling drunk—and she goes and drinks again. So they can't stop."

Although from her words it is evident that the two

of them figure in exactly identical rôles, nevertheless the old lady always concludes that *she* is to blame.

"Quit it!" she says to the landlord. "Stop, I tell you! You brought that hay worth a hundred rubles—three hundred versts you brought it, and there it lies out in the rain on the boats. The boss is drunk, and the workers just fool around. Everything is going to smash."

Then, changing her tone to one of compassion, the old lady continues:

"I know it is bitter for you! She drinks all the time; she is no housekeeper—good-for-nothing!"

And here the landlord himself, a tall *moujik* with twisty, dirty hair hanging over his face, sitting solemnly on a bench and only half sobered up, begins in a repentant, broken, whimpering voice:

"Yes, you might say that, gra'mother . . . to drink that way. . . . That hay now. . . . Well, you take a look at it, gra'mother. . . . Everlastingly drinking. . . . I should think that would burn up the heart. . . . You can't eat or drink. . . . Why, the gentleman himself had to fetch water from the river. . . . I was jigged out of four twenty-five ruble notes. . . . Such things never happen. . . . What shall we do with her, gra'mother? There the mare lies, dead drunk. . . . How long, Maria, will you keep on drinking?" He turns suddenly on his wife. "I *ask* you!"

Here begins an ugly scene. The landlord drags his wife out of the cottage, and the old lady follows, slowly bringing forward one foot after the other, bending over, stretching out her left hand for equilibrium and feeling her way with a long, thin staff in her right hand. The landlord beats his wife ferociously, pronouncing a string of meaningless imprecations. His wife, still completely drunk, grabs with one hand at the old lady, who slowly falls.

I hear a senile cry:

"Oh, they are killing me! The brigands are killing me!"

I run out there and lift up the old lady, who steadily continues to assert that they are killing her. My presence embarrasses the landlord. He stands tall and disheveled with hands spread out helplessly, and after I have set the old lady on the bench begins to repeat:

"We dropped gra'mother. . . . Mister, lift gra'-mother up. . . . Please, mister, lift up. . . . We dropped the old lady. You, please, mister, lift her up!"

After that the landlord disappears, to come back in about an hour completely drunk again. His wife employs this intermediate time by running to me in my room, putting in my hand a twenty-five ruble note—probably one of those stolen from the landlord. Intoxicated, bruised, her shirt torn and her breast naked, she begins to beseech me in a wailing, tearful-drunken voice:

"Be my own father! Go out, for the love of God, and buy me a little bottle."

All Urgutsk seems to me at this moment a drunken pit without exit, a prison surrounded with that stockade of jungle trees. . . .

Trotsky's pen is alive in these writings. They tempt you to say that the world lost in him a literary artist. The world found in him one genuinely creative man who could not be tempted away from action.

> I am yours, my friends, I will be yours,
> Ready for labor and the sword,
> So in our union there begin
> A living deed and not a word.

He quotes this from the poetry of Dobroliubov, and it tells his real thoughts better than anything else in these censored articles.

CHAPTER VIII

A SOCIAL-DEMOCRATIC party had been formed in Russia while Trotsky was fighting lice in the prison of Kherzon. But that party was little more than a constitution and manifesto. Practically all the delegates to the first convention had been arrested, as well as all the leading workers all over Russia. There remained merely the idea of a Marxian party, and widely scattered little groups of people, in jail, in exile, in hiding, ardently debating the problems of its tactics.

They were debating two questions in particular. One was whether the party should explicitly and immediately advocate a political struggle culminating in the overthrow of the czar, or whether it should confine its attention to the economic struggle of the workers, postponing the political issue or leaving it in the hands of the bourgeoisie. Upon this question Trotsky had already taken his stand in the Nikolaev days. He had no instinct for post-

139

ponement. The revolution is political as well as economic, he said, and its first task is to overthrow the czar.

The other great question of debate among those Marxians was whether the party ought to be a centralized organization, commanded by its executive committee as an army is by its general staff, or whether it ought to be a very democratic federation of local groups with their own independent treasury and autonomous executive. Upon this question, in the Nikolaev days, Trotsky had taken the impractical view. His instincts were democratic, and as we have seen he was a rather Utopian conspirator.

But experience and reflection and his long study of Marxism had made him wiser. He argued against these diluters of the revolution now—the "Economists" as they were called—not only on the issue of political agitation, but also on the issue of centralization. When he visited Irkutsk in the spring of 1902 he made a speech before the Social-Democratic circle there which is still remembered as an impetuous assault upon the weak, disintegrating and counter-revolutionary tendencies of this prevailing group. Trotsky had not only mastered the science of Marxism and the art of writing during his four years of peace, but he had taken long steps toward becoming a practical engineer of history, a Bolshevik.

Trotsky brought back with him from Irkutsk some copies of the new journal, "Iskra," in which Lenin was annihilating "Economism" with his sledge-hammer of logic and fact and calling for the organization of an "all-Russian organization of professional revolutionarists." It was a journal founded in London upon the initiative of Lenin, but with the coöperation of five other revolutionary leaders—Plechanov, Martov, Axelrod, Potriesov and Vera Zassulitch.

The foundation of that journal was a momentous event in the history of human culture, and its creeping into the little far-off Siberian city, after a year and a half of secret traveling, was a momentous event in Trotsky's life. He was restless already. He had finished his education. His trip to Irkutsk had been the expression of an impatient impulse, a feeling for the path that should lead him back into his life's work. Lenin showed him the path. An all-Russian organization of professional revolutionarists—that was where he belonged. And it was in order to go to Lenin and put himself at the service of that organization that he made his escape from Siberia.

> I am yours, my friends, I will be yours,
> Ready for Labor and the sword,
> So in our union there begin
> A living deed, and not a word!

Trotsky and Alexandra Lvovna lived in a little two-story house in Verkholensk, and in the evenings after they had put the babies to bed downstairs they went up into the second story to read and study. They went up a ladder and through a trap-door in the ceiling, and they closed the door after them. Every evening at about ten o'clock, while they sat there reading, this door would slowly rise from the floor, and the big, red-whiskered face and watery blue eyes of their police inspector would peer silently around the room and then silently disappear again as the door descended into place. This event always made Trotsky mad, and one night he jumped off his chair and gave a lunge with his foot at that disappearing face.

"Don't ever show your face above this floor again!" he said.

It was a preposterous thing to say, a command delivered in circumstances where a bribe would have been more appropriate. But Trotsky has a peculiar genius, as we have already observed, which consists in the fact that his commands are obeyed. That face never appeared above the floor again, and five days later Trotsky's absence from the village was discovered accidentally by the chief of police. Trotsky had ridden away, buried under the straw in a peasant's wagon, and now he was in Irkutsk, disguised and supplied with a passport and buying a railroad ticket to Samara.

Trotsky's passport, supplied by the underground organization at Irkutsk, was a carelessly forged blank which he himself had to fill out. It was a vain thing for safety, but it gave him the opportunity, which a great many people might enjoy, of choosing his own name. He could never be Leon Bronstein again in Russia —and moreover in the existing circumstances he could not be a Jew. For Jews, except as convicts and condemned exiles, were legally debarred by the czar's government from Siberia. Trotsky borrowed his name from the head keeper of the prison where he had lived in Odessa, and he chose it not only because he liked it, but because from the standpoint of race it seemed noncommittal.

Samara was the Russian headquarters for the distribution of "Iskra," and Trotsky carried a letter from the circle in Irkutsk to Glyeb Krizhanovsky, the head of the Russian organization. He presented it in the summer of 1902. To Krizhanovsky thus fell the task of deciding what Trotsky should do—whether he should travel to London and serve as a writer, or whether he should stay in Russia as an organizer. As Trotsky is probably both the best writer and the best organizer that the Socialist movement ever produced, this decision could not have been an easy one for Krizhanovsky.

He began by sending Trotsky on a mission of persuasion to Kiev and Poltava. He was to find centers there for the distribution of "Iskra" and local correspondents for the paper, and he was to establish an underground connection between these two cities and Samara. In Poltava there was a group of workers wavering between Economism and the policies of "Iskra," and a part of Trotsky's task was to win them over. He was to persuade them to send delegates to the coming convention of the party, for which the "Iskra" group were acting as an organizing committee. Trotsky fulfilled all these tasks with adequate success and without having to display his dubious passport, and he returned to Samara for further orders.

Krizhanovsky had decided in the meantime that Trotsky was a writer and should go to headquarters—a decision which he revoked soon after, and wrote to headquarters asking that Trotsky should be sent back to Russia as an organizer.   He christened Trotsky with the party nickname of "Piero"—the Russian word for pen—and supplied him with a railroad ticket to the Austrian border, and enough money to get him thence to Zurich, where lived Axelrod, the nearest of the six editors of "Iskra."

On account of the imperfections of his passport Trotsky arranged his departure from Samara with a good deal of care.   A young student named Soloviev, whose apartment he had shared, took his bags to the station and got on the train with them.   The plan was that Soloviev should sit there in the car until the very last moment, when Trotsky would rush in with just barely time to catch the train, and then Soloviev would withdraw.   Trotsky would thus be on board with his baggage without having had to linger in the station or pass slowly through the gates which were so well watched by the czar's police.

This plan worked admirably up to the point when Trotsky was supposed to rush in at the last moment and catch the train. At that point Trotsky was off in the by-streets taking a walk, having been told at the station that the train would be an hour late. He heard the whistle and ran all the way to the station; but he arrived just in time to see the train moving off and his friend Soloviev sitting among his bags in the middle of the track. He was trying to explain to a large public, including all the police officers and detectives in the station, just why he had jumped up and tumbled off the train the moment it started, with passengers, who naturally thought he was a maniac, hanging on to his coat tails. Trotsky sneaked out of the station and went home in a hurry. And after another evening of hilarious laughter with his friends in Samara, he left town without any elaborate preparations.

His trip was uneventful until he reached the little village of Kamenets Podolsk on the Austrian border, where revolutionists and revolutionary writings were smuggled in and out of Russia, along with other merchandise, by the poor Jewish trading population. The price for passing over a "comrade" was fixed and well understood. It was eleven rubles. Trotsky knew that the price was eleven rubles; nevertheless he paid twenty-five—not out of philanthropic intentions, but just because he is an "easy mark."

Whether it is a survival in him of the conscience of his childhood, when he used to feel guilty of the wealth of his parents, or whether it is merely his natural generosity, it is a fact that Trotsky can never be trusted to carry the money. He can not get through any form of polite hold-up work from anybody who does anything for him, with a cent in his pocket.

He knew quite well that the young student who engineered his transfer, kept him waiting two days in his bedroom while a mysterious cargo of "literature" was being passed over, merely in order to impress him with the momentousness of the enterprise. He knew quite well that he was carried across the river in a deep place on a man's back and given a good soaking in order further to impress him with the services he was paying for. He *saw* a place where he could have crossed the river wading only up to his knees.

And he knew that the old Jewish peasant with a horse and sulky and a rooster tied by the legs, who drove him at midnight into an Austrian village, entertained him in hoarse whispers with tales of the danger they were running, the probability of being shot when they crossed certain bridges, with the same commercial purpose. Just before they reached one of these most dangerous bridges, the old man went astray in the dark, and his wheel slipped into a ditch. The sulky tipped over, and he and Trotsky and the rooster were all dumped out into a mud puddle. The rooster was pinned under the wheel, and screamed and cackled hysterically.

"Kill him! Can't you kill him?" Trotsky whispered fiercely.

"I can't find him!" whispered the old man, groping about in the dark. "Besides I can't kill him—he has to be killed by a *schocket*."

Trotsky smiled grimly and helped the old man to right the sulky. The rooster continued to advertise their arrival at intervals all the way into town, but there was no shooting. There were no questions asked. There was no sign of life anywhere. All these things Trotsky observed and understood and commented upon within his own ironical mind.

But when it came to paying the money, he had no power of resistance. He gave each of these experts twice as much as he was supposed to and got on the train for Vienna without a cent left of what Krizhanovsky had given him for the journey to Zurich.

Trotsky was hungry when he arrived in Vienna, but he was not worried. His arrival was that of a Russian revolutionary leader escaping from Siberia, and his only problem was to make this momentous fact known to the leaders of the Austrian Social Democracy—to Victor Adler, for instance. That was the state of his feelings. You will never know Trotsky if you do not know what it is to feel important and absolutely self-confident. He managed to get hold of a copy of Victor Adler's paper, the *Arbeiter Zeitung,* without paying for it, and he managed after some wandering to arrive at the address printed on it.

A sedate and severe intellectual with two pairs of glasses on was coming down the stairs. It was Austerlitz, the editor-in-chief.

"Excuse me," said Trotsky in very bad German, "but I must see Comrade Adler."

The editor-in-chief paused and examined him through his glasses.

"The *Herr Doktor?*" he corrected.

"Yes."

"Impossible!" he exploded. "Impossible!"

"But let me explain who I am," said Trotsky. "I am a Russian revolutionist escaped from Siberia, and I am on my way——"

"It wouldn't make any difference if you came to announce that you had assassinated the czar, you can not see the *Herr Doktor* on Sunday!"

Trotsky managed to extract from Austerlitz the *Herr Doktor's* home address, however, and he presented himself there, subdued but not conquered. The doctor himself came to the door, and Trotsky recognized him from his pictures. He too was severe, and when Trotsky began to apologize for arriving uninvited on Sunday, he interrupted with an impatient:

"Ja! Weiter, weiter!"

But there was kindness in his eyes, and while Trotsky was trying to find some German words to explain his situation, the doctor turned and called into the house:

"Katia!"

A young Russian girl appeared in answer to his call, and the doctor said:

"Now it will go better!"

It did go better. It went so well that Trotsky stayed some days in the house of Victor Adler, receiving quite as warm a welcome as his self-confidence had predicted and being supplied on his departure with twenty-five crowns for the rest of his journey to Zurich.

It was an ample sum. But again there were porters, there were conductors, waiters. There were panhandlers. There were bookstalls. And Trotsky arrived in Zurich once more without a cent in his pocket. He arrived in the middle of the night. . . .

I remember the first impression I had of Trotsky's character. I got it from an American journalist, who told me that Trotsky was a "queer irresponsible sort of a guy," so very "communistic" that when he arrived in a strange town, he would go and knock at the door of the first house he saw and order the people to pay for his taxi and put him up! Trotsky is so entirely opposite to that, so punctilious about money matters, and with such a very keen sense of privacy too, that I wondered what was the source of the story. . . . I found it here. He took a taxicab that night in Zurich straight to Axelrod's house, routed him up at two o'clock in the morning and said:

"Please pay for the cab, and afterward I will explain to you what it is about."

There is something almost ludicrous in Trotsky's self-confidence. Those who do not like him call it self-importance. But that is not right, for it is an instinctive attitude, not a result of reflection. Trotsky has, to be sure, that sense of self and its rights and dignities that proud people have—a trait that goes better in a feudal than a proletarian society—but this does not mean that he thinks about his own importance. My opinion is that Trotsky thinks about himself very little. He does not like to think about himself. He tried to read a page of this book once and shoved it away in disgust. "It makes me uncomfortable," he said.

In conversation with him my continual difficulty has been to get him to relate his own experiences and not tell me the life-stories of all his friends. I doubt if there are many famous people who, in the same circumstances, would reveal the same weakness.

Axelrod gave Trotsky some more money and started him on his way to London by way of Paris. It took Trotsky two months to get from Paris to London, and as we are describing him as a young man upon a pilgrimage of consecration it is necessary to pause a moment and explain this fact. There was always a colony of Russian revolutionary exiles in Paris, and in this colony, as elsewhere, "Iskra" had its own group.

This group had a kind of unofficial committee of welcome for new emigrants and exiles from Russia, and the head of this committee for the moment was Natalia Ivanovna Siedova. She was a strong-hearted, quiet girl with high cheek-bones and eyes a little sad—a girl of noble birth, who had been a rebel since childhood. From a young ladies' boarding-school in Kharkov, where she had persuaded her whole class to refuse to attend prayers and to read Chernishevsky instead of the Bible, she had gone to Moscow University and from there to Geneva, seeking knowledge and revolutionary companionship. And in the circle surrounding Plechanov in Geneva she had found them both. She had become a member of the organization of "Iskra," and had already made one trip into Russia, carrying illegal literature, when Trotsky met her in Paris.

Her task of welcoming emigrants consisted chiefly of finding them cheap rooms to live in and leading them to the cheapest restaurants. And the room she had found for Trotsky was little more than a cupboard opening on an air-shaft. She had been arranging it for him, and was coming down the stairs when he met her. . . .

I imagine there were enough romances in Trotsky's life at this period to occupy a really conscientious biographer for several chapters. He had lost all that diffidence concealed by roughness which characterized his boyish relations with girls—or he had retained just enough of it to make his charms most fatal. And he belonged, to judge by the fame which he retains in the minds of those who knew him then, to the school of Engels, and not of Marx, in this important matter. Therefore it is not a very significant fact that he fell in love with Natalia Ivanovna when he met her on the stairs coming down from his room on the air-shaft. But it is significant that he formed with her a friendship so deep and understanding that they have lived together all their lives, and that he loves her now.

Natalia Ivanovna is not Trotsky's wife, if you have a perfectly legal American mind, for Trotsky was never divorced from Alexandra Lvovna, who still uses the name of Bronstein. Natalia Ivanovna is Trotsky's best and dearest friend, his daily companion. She is the mother of his sons. . . . And to sum up a number of things that are not the business of a contemporary biographer — Alexandra Lvovna is also his friend.

CHAPTER IX

LENIN AND TROTSKY

AFTER two happy months in Paris Trotsky went on with his pilgrimage to Lenin. He has himself described, in a little book about "Lenin and the Early 'Iskra,'" how they first met. I will quote from that book, as it is the most authentic account of this period of Trotsky's life.

But to make the picture that it gives complete the reader must know that Lenin loved Trotsky. He took him wholly into his heart with that union of revolutionary admiration and personal affection which was the romantic motive in his life. He recognized Trotsky's magnificent powers instantly, and with such confidence that he was only prevented by Plechanov from making him one of the editors of "Iskra."

I arrived in London [Trotsky writes] in the autumn of 1902—it must have been October—early in the morning. A cab, engaged by the method of gesticulation, delivered me at an address written on a slip of paper, my ultimate destination. That was the apartment of Vladimir Ilych. I had already learned—it must have been in Zurich—to knock the proper number of times at the door.

The door was opened, as I remember, by Nadiezhda Konstantinovna,* whom I suppose I had roused out of bed with my knocking. The hour was early, and any experienced person, anyone accustomed, as you might say, to civilized social life, would have sat still at the station for a couple of hours instead of knocking before dawn at a strange door. But I was still loaded full of my successful escape from Verkholensk. In practically the same way I had routed up the household of Axelrod in Zurich, only not at dawn, but in the middle of the night.

Vladimir Ilych was still in bed, and the welcome in his face was mingled with a legitimate perplexity. In those circumstances occurred our first meeting and our first conversation. Both Vladimir Ilych and Nadiezhda Konstantinovna knew about me already from the letter of Krizhanovsky, who had officially enrolled me in the organization of "Iskra" under the nickname of "Piero." So I was met this way:

"Well, Piero has come."

. . . They poured me some tea in the kitchen-dining-room. And meanwhile Vladimir Ilych dressed himself. I told about my escape and complained of the bad condition of the "Iskra" frontier; it was in the hands of a high-school student, a Social-Revolutionary who looked

---

* Lenin's wife.

upon the *Iskrovtsi*, thanks to the cruel polemic blazing
up between them, with small sympathy; moreover the
smugglers held me up cruelly, raising all tariffs and
established standards. To Nadiezhda Konstantinovna
I gave my modest baggage of names and addresses,
exact information as to the necessity of abandoning
certain useless addresses. . . .

I don't remember whether it was the same day or
the next morning that Vladimir Ilych and I took a long
walk through London. He showed me Westminster
Abbey (from the outside) and certain other eminent
buildings. I don't remember what he said, but the
shading of it was:

"That's a fine Westminster of theirs."

Of theirs meant, of course, not of the English, but
of the enemy. That shading, not in the least empha-
sized, deeply organic, expressed mostly in the timbre
of his voice, was always noticeable in Vladimir Ilych
when he spoke of some treasures of culture or some new
achievement—of the structure of the British Museum,
of the wealth of information in the "Times"—or many
years after, of the German artillery or French avia-
tion; they can or they ken, they have made or achieved
—but what enemies! The invisible shadow of the ex-
ploiting class rested in his eyes upon all human culture, and he perceived that shadow always, and with
the same indubitability as the light of day.

As far as I remember, I bestowed at that time upon
London architecture a minimum of attention. Tossed
all at once from Verkholensk beyond the border, where
I was arriving for the first time, I took in Vienna,

Paris, London, only in the most summary fashion. I had no time for "details" such as the Westminster Cathedral. Yes, and it was not for this that Vladimir Ilych had invited me on that long walk. His object was to get acquainted, to give me an examination. And the examination was indeed "on the whole course. . . ."

As to my further work the conversation was at that time of course very general. I wanted first of all to get acquainted with the literature which had already appeared, and afterward I assumed that I would return illegally into Russia. It was decided that I ought in the first place to "look around a bit."

For lodging Nadiezhda Konstantinovna led me several blocks away to a house where lived Zassulitch and Martov and Blumenfield, who managed the typographical side of "Iskra." There was a free room there for me. That apartment was arranged, according to the customary English style, not horizontally but vertically. In the lowest room lived the landlady and then, one above the other, the tenants. There was one free sitting room which Plechanov christened the "den." In that room, thanks largely to Vera Ivanovna Zassulitch, but not without the coöperation of Martov, there reigned an enormous disorder. Here we drank coffee, smoked, came together for conversation.

Here began the short London period of my life. I devoured greedily the numbers of "Iskra" which had already appeared, and the little magazine "Zaria." At that time I began my contributions to "Iskra." For the two hundredth anniversary of the Schlusselburg

Fortress I wrote a small article, my first work, it seems, for "Iskra." My article ended with Homer's words, or rather the words of Homer's translator Gniedich, referring to the "hands unvanquished" which the revolution will lay on czarism. (I had been reading the Iliad in the train on my way from Siberia.) Lenin liked my article, but as to the "hands unvanquished" he felt a legitimate doubt and expressed it to me with a good-natured smile.

"Yes, that is a line from Homer," I justified myself.

But I willingly agreed that a classic quotation was not obligatory. You can find my small article in "Iskra," but without the "hands unvanquished."

At that time also I made my first speech in White-chapel, where I came into conflict with the "old man" Chaikovsky—he was even then an old man—and with the anarchist Cherekiesov, also not young. I was sincerely astonished that eminent, gray-bearded emigrants could talk such obvious nonsense. . . .

During my stay in London Plechanov came for a short visit, and I went to see him the first evening. In the little room, besides Plechanov, sat a fairly well-known German writer, a Social-Democrat, Baer, and the Englishman Askew. Not knowing where to put me, since there were no more chairs, Plechanov—not without hesitation—proposed that I should sit on the bed. I considered this to be in the usual order of things, not guessing that Plechanov—a European to his finger-tips—could only in the most extreme circumstances decide upon such an extraordinary measure. The conversation was conducted in the German language, with which Plechanov was insufficiently acquainted, and therefore it was limited to monosyllabic remarks. . . .

Baer and Askew soon departed. George Valentinovitch, with ample justification, expected that I would depart with them, since the hour was late and we ought not to disturb the landlady with conversation. I, on the contrary, considered that the real thing was only just beginning.

"Baer said some interesting things," I remarked.

"Yes, as to English politics interesting, but as to philosophy nonsense," answered Plechanov.

Seeing that I did not intend to withdraw, he offered me a neighborly glass of beer. He put me a few idle questions, was agreeable enough; but in his agreeableness there was a shade of hidden impatience. I felt that his attention wandered. It is possible that he was merely tired after the day. But I left him with a feeling of dissatisfaction and hurt. . . .

One Sunday Vladimir Ilych and Nadiezhda Konstantinovna and I went to a Socialistic church in London, where a Social-Democratic meeting alternated with the singing of revolutionary-pious psalms. The orator was a typesetter who had returned to his native land, it seems, from Australia. Vladimir Ilych translated his speech to us in a whisper, and it seemed revolutionary enough, at least for those times. Afterward everybody stood up and sang: "Almighty God, do something so there will not be any more kings and rich people!" or something of that kind.

It is needless to say that Vladimir Ilych lived more

than modestly with Nadiezhda Konstantinovna and her mother. Returning from the Social-Democratic church, we dined in the little kitchen-dining-room of their two-room apartment. I remember, as though it were now, the slices of fried meat served in a frying-pan. We drank tea and joked as always about the question whether I would be able to find my way home alone. . . .

After my "trial speech," as you might call it, at Whitechapel, they sent me for a tour on the Continent—to Brussels, Liège, Paris. My speech was on the subject: "What Is Historic Materialism, and How Do the Social-Revolutionaries Understand It?" Vladimir Ilych was much interested in the theme. I gave him a detailed outline to look over, with citations and so forth. He advised me to work up the speech in the form of an article for the coming number of "Zaria," but I lacked the courage.

From Paris they summoned me quickly back to London by telegram. It was a question of sending me illegally into Russia—Vladimir Ilych's idea. There were complaints from Russia about arrests, a lack of workers, and it seems Krizhanovsky had asked for my return. But before I had time to reach London the plan was changed. A. G. Deich, who was living then in London, and was very kindly disposed to me, told me subsequently how he "interceded" for me, arguing that "the youth" (he never spoke of me otherwise) needed to live a little abroad and educate himself, and how Lenin after a certain amount of opposition had agreed to this. I was allured by the idea of working in the Russian organization of "Iskra," but I nevertheless willingly stayed for a certain time abroad.

In the London period, as also later in Geneva, I was with Zassulitch and Martov far oftener than with Lenin. Living in London in the same apartment, and in Geneva lunching and dining in the same restaurants, Martov and Zassulitch and I met several times a day, whereas with Lenin, who took his meals at home, each meeting outside the official conferences was already something of a little event. . . .

Before the great convention of the party, which was held in London in the summer of 1903, the office of "Iskra" was transferred to Geneva, and all the preparations for the convention, and the preliminary conferences of the delegates, were conducted there. Trotsky was "sent to Paris" on his way to Geneva—he succeeded in being sent to Paris, it seems, every once in a while—and he and Natalia Ivanovna went to Geneva together. Of the days in Geneva he relates some further things that belong as much to his own biography as to Lenin's:

The sharpest question for Lenin [he says] was how to organize for the future the central organ of the party, which was going to be practically also the Central Committee. Lenin considered it impossible to preserve the old group of six. Zassulitch and Axelrod upon a disputed question almost invariably took the side of Plechanov, and thus at the best you had a deadlock of three against three. Neither group would agree to remove someone from the Collegium. There remained the opposite course, to enlarge the Collegium. Lenin wanted to introduce me as a seventh member, with the idea that from the seven as a broad editorial board he would separate out a narrower editorial group consisting of Lenin, Plechanov and Martov. Lenin made me acquainted with this plan gradually and without saying a word of the fact that it was I he had proposed as a seventh member of the editorial board and that this proposition had been accepted by all except Plechanov, in whose person the whole plan encountered a decisive resistance. The very inclusion of a seventh member meant in the eyes of Plechanov a retirement of his group; it meant four "young ones" against three "old."

I think that this plan was the most important cause of George Valentinovitch's very unfavorable attitude to me. But to increase it there were other little open conflicts of ours before the delegates. These began, it seems, upon the question of a popular journal. Certain delegates insisted on the necessity of establishing alongside of "Iskra" a popular organ—so far as such a thing was possible in Russia. . . .

Lenin was decidedly opposed to this plan. His reasons were various, but the principal one was the danger of a special grouping which might form itself upon the basis of a popular simplification of the ideas of the social democracy before the fundamental nucleus of the party had become sufficiently strong. Plechanov spoke decisively for the formation of the popular organ, opposing Lenin and clearly seeking support among the delegates. I supported Lenin. In one of the conferences I developed the idea—rightly or wrongly, it does not matter now—that what we needed was not a popular organ, but a series of propaganda brochures and leaflets which would help the advanced workers to raise themselves to the level of "Iskra"; that a popular journal would supplant "Iskra" and blur the political physiognomy of the party, reducing it to Economism, etc. Plechanov objected.

"Why blur it?" he said. "Obviously in a popular organ we cannot say everything. We will advance demands there, slogans, and not occupy ourselves with questions of tactics. We will say to the workers that it is necessary to struggle with capitalism, but we will not, of course, theorize as to how to struggle with capitalism."

I seized upon that argument.

"But the Economists and Social-Revolutionaries say that it is necessary to struggle with capitalism! The difference between us begins exactly there—how to struggle. If in a popular organ we do not answer that question we *ipso facto* blur the distinction between us and the Social-Revolutionaries!"

My answer had a very triumphant look. Plechanov found nothing to say. Obviously this episode did not improve his attitude to me. . . .

Trotsky describes another of these conflicts in

which Lenin supported him against Plechanov,
and he continues:

In both these instances the sympathy of Vladimir
Ilych was, as we see, upon my side. But at the same
time he observed with alarm how my relations with
Plechanov were becoming spoiled—a thing which
threatened final destruction to his plan for reorganiz-
ing the editorship. In one of the next conferences with
newly arrived delegates Lenin, leading me aside, said
to me:

"On the question about a popular organ, better let
Martov answer Plechanov. Martov will lubricate the
thing, but you will start chopping. Better let him
lubricate!"

Those expressions *chop* and *lubricate* I clearly remember.

Trotsky may well remember those expressions, for they point to the one thing which pre-
vents him from being a great political leader.
Lenin called it "excessive self-confidence," but
Trotsky's self-confidence is not greater than that
of Lenin. What Trotsky lacks is a sense of the
feelings of the other man—an immediate sense
that is not a matter of reflection and that would
guide him unconsciously to those words and ges-
tures which center the attention upon objective
issues and not upon personal relations. When

Trotsky triumphs, it always has a "triumphant look." When Lenin triumphs, it is just the truth, and nobody is disturbed. Trotsky is too full of himself—not in a vain way, although many people mistakenly think so—but he is too full of his own will and his own passion to orient himself tactfully in a group. For that reason, while he is great as a commander and inspirer—and also as a thinker—he is not great as a leader of men.

CHAPTER X

AS you see, Lenin was clearly aware long before the convention of a line dividing him from his older associates. He had long ceased to try to regard himself as a pupil of Plechanov. He must have seen almost immediately the lack of dynamic force in that man. And he was beginning to see the same thing in Martov. He was already forming in his mind that division between the "hard" and the "soft," between the "workers" and "gabblers," the "fighters" and "reasoners"—between Bolsheviks and Mensheviks—which was his great fundamental contribution to the science of revolution.

It was in the last analysis a psychological contribution. For although it is an economic fact that makes Mensheviks dangerous to the revolution—the fact that they express in their mental attitude the equivocal economic interests of the *petit-bourgeois* class and the aristocracy of labor—it is not class interest that makes them Mensheviks. They belong with the Bolsheviks to the class of the intelligentsia, the revolutionary idealists, and what makes them Mensheviks is their attitude toward ideas.

It is impossible to understand Trotsky's life, or indeed the political life of our times, without clearly defining this distinction between two different types of intellectuals, which Lenin's policies have forced into the consciousness and the language of mankind. It is not a distinction merely among Marxists or the advocates of a proletarian revolution; it is a distinction that can be made wherever human beings gather together upon the basis of belief in an idea.

The belief in ideas has two contrary functions in our emotional life, and those in whom it fulfills one function will inevitably divide at the moment of action with those in whom it fulfills the other. We erect an idea in our minds because we are ill at ease or at pain in the circumstances of reality. The original function of the idea was to guide us in an effort to change the reality fundamentally and so get relief. But in order to fulfill this function the idea itself must have for us a certain reality. We must be able to love it, linger upon it, adhere to it in social groups, sacrifice our time and money, and even our respectability, to its cultivation. And in this process we often manage to alleviate the pain of the reality without changing it fundamentally. We do this with the greater ease if we are "intellectual" and ideas are very real to us. They become a kind of daily companion and redeemer of our world, consoling us with an extreme "belief" about its future and yet leaving us free to patch it up in little ways less disturbing and more ready to our hand.

It is obvious that while employing an idea in this latter fashion, we shall resent any attempt to rob that idea of its purity, which is essentially its mentality. We shall resent with equal violence an attempt to prove that the idea is incapable of realization and an attempt actually to realize it—because either of these attempts, if successful, will destroy its value as an object of devout attention, a love and consolation in the pain and ugliness of what is real.

Plato, the first Communist, was an intellectual of this static type. But he was conscious of the fact, and boldly declared that ideas were more interesting and more real to him than things. He had no method, and he had no need of a method, for realizing his Ideal Republic. The modern Menshevik is not conscious of his character. He has not the bold mysticism of

Plato, and he *has* a method for realizing his ideal. The method as well as the ideal enters into the substance of his belief. It is a belief about a real future.

And when that method begins to be actually applied, when that future begins to show its harsh substance in the present, this unconscious Platonist finds himself in a very embarrassing position. He has solved his problem of life by *believing in* an idea. He has perhaps made it his profession to believe in that idea. And he is compelled in defense of his vital equilibrium, in defense of his very personality—for the belief is deep and sincere—to resist those who undertake to put the idea into action. He is compelled to play the part of hypocrite. But he is not a hypocrite; he is something far more complex and pitiable than that. He is a Menshevik.

It was his sense of this psychological truth, and the marvelous accuracy with which he could drive a line between these two types of intellectuals, that made Lenin's actions so startling during and immediately after this first gathering of leaders for the Russian revolution. He had already annihilated Economism and united a big majority around the banner of "Iskra." But he did not hesitate to go ahead and split this majority again upon the question—essentially—of the relation of intellectuals to the party organization.

Shall idealistic-minded people who give merely money and formal adherence—not disciplined service, risk, personal sacrifice—be considered members of the party? That was the issue upon which the convention split and upon which Lenin in the long run was willing to break with his best political friends, the five other editors of "Iskra," including his great theoretical supporter, Plechanov. For these editors, being of the Menshevik type, instinctively defended the rights of that type in the party constitution. Lenin threw them off, broke with them personally as well as politically—for politics was his life—and went on without their authority, building up that body of dynamic intellectuals whom history has christened with the name of Bolsheviks.

And what became of our altogether dynamic youth, Trotsky, in this startling turn of events? If I have told the reader anything in this book, I have told him that Trotsky is a Bolshevik. Trotsky means action down to the last letter of every word that comes out of his mouth. And Lenin knew that. He considered Trotsky, as we have seen, one of his men, one of the inevitable leaders of the Russian revolution. The relation between them in the first sessions of the convention is indicated in the fact that Trotsky received the nickname among the delegates of "Lenin's Big Stick."

But Trotsky was innocent as a child of the sharpening division which existed among the editors of "Iskra." He thought that they were a perfect and harmonious intellectual family. His first speech at the convention, which was greeted with storms of applause, was a defense of the proposal to "confirm" this journal as the central organ of the new party. It was a brilliant summing up of the revolutionary history of the preceding decade, a demonstration of the achievement of "Iskra" and a warm, glowing, youthful, wholesale tribute to it and to its editors without distinction.

"It is not only the name that we confirm today," he cried, "it is the banner, the banner around which in actual fact our party united!"

That was the mood in which Trotsky attended the convention—a mood of ardent and indiscriminating admiration for this sacred group, who were assembling the real Marxians—the scientific fighters, as he thought—who would go ahead and achieve the Russian revolution: Plechanov, the great, sharp-minded scholar and father of Russian Marxism; Vera Zassulitch, the heroine of the Terror, who had shot the czar's prime minister for having her comrades flogged and yet afterward had become a Marxist; Martov, the most fluent and capable revolutionary journalist in Russia; Axelrod, for whose "sincere and simple" hospitality Trotsky still has a word of appreciation in his little book about those times; and Lenin, who was already the dominant figure in the group. It is no wonder that Trotsky was carried away with admiration for this galaxy and unable to consider the possibility of a serious discord among them.

"I swallowed 'Iskra' whole," he says, "and it was alien to me, and even a kind of inwardly hostile thought, to seek in it, or its editors, any different tendencies, shades, influences.

"I remember I noticed that certain leading articles and *feuilletons* in 'Iskra,' although they were not signed, employed the pronoun 'I': 'In such a number I said'; 'I already spoke of this in such and such a number,' etc. I asked whose these articles were. They proved to be all Lenin's. In conversation with him I remarked that in my opinion it was awkward from a lit-

erary standpoint to use the pronoun 'I' in un-
signed articles.

" 'Why awkward?' he asked with interest, sup-
posing perhaps that I was not expressing my
own or a casual opinion.

" 'Oh, it just seems so,' I answered vaguely,
for I had no clearly defined thoughts on the
matter.

" 'I don't find it so,' Lenin said, and smiled
in a kind of enigmatic way. . . . The signaliz-
ing of his articles, although they were not
signed, was a measure of insurance for his line
of thought, due to a lack of confidence in that
of his closest colleagues."

Now, if you will add to this mood of Trotsky
—the wholesale devotion to a solidarity which
did not exist—the fact that he lived with Martov
and Zassulitch, and all his unconscious growth
was under their influence, while his meetings
with Vladimir Ilych were "something of a little
event," you will begin to understand imagina-
tively why he sided with the Mensheviks at the
beginning of that split. His own character was
wholly Bolshevik, and he had faith in his friends.
He had faith in people that seemed to be like
him—in the general run of bourgeois intellectuals who become "sincere Marxists."

He was, and is, a bad psychologist in so far as psychology means a penetrating sensitiveness to the dispositions of others. He felt in the first place that Lenin was making a great to-do about a matter of no vital consequence. He opposed Lenin on the floor of the convention in this spirit, and with a very poor speech. And then afterward, when Lenin's break with Martov took a personal form, he was personally incensed. He saw that sacred solidarity of "Iskra" breaking down, and he saw Lenin, in what seemed a wantonly dictatorial spirit, breaking it down.

Maxim Litvinov told me that Trotsky came to him in Geneva during the period after the convention, seeking to win him over to the position of the Mensheviks, and the principal burden of his argument was that "Lenin had insulted Martov." Trotsky was young then; he was only twenty-four. And proud people who are full of self-confidence grow up very slowly. A humble man might have been older at twenty.

The split arose specifically upon the adoption of the first paragraph of the constitution of the party. The paragraph offered by Lenin proposed that only those should be considered members of the party who "recognize the program and support the party, not only financially, but by personal participation in one of its organizations." Martov wanted to substitute for "personal participation" the "more elastic" idea of "regular coöperation with" the party, "under the control" of one of its organizations. Trotsky regarded this distinction, just as the uninitiated reader doubtless will, as a matter of no great importance, and he took the side of Martov.

"I am far from giving the constitution a mystic significance," he said. "Lenin . . . wants to make it a constricting noose for those politically corrupt and corrupting denizens of the 'cultured circles' who call themselves Social-Democrats in order to assemble the youth and turn them over to Peter Struve.* Believe me, comrades, I would be the first to grasp any formula which would be a noose for these ladies and gentlemen. . . . But what is to prevent them from entering into any broad party organization? . . . And what is the sense, I say, in restricting the rights of those solitary intellectuals who

---

* The most notorious of the "Economists." He opened his career by writing one of the first "expositions" of Marxism in the Russian language, and closed it as a political lieutenant of Baron Wrangel in the Crimea.

stand on the principles of the party program and do service in solitude under the guidance of the organization?"

That was the character of Trotsky's first opposition to Lenin. His enemies like to quote this remark about "solitary intellectuals" and declare that it reveals a "knightly anarchism" which is organically unable to reconcile itself to the narrow frame of organization and party discipline. The real psychology of Trotsky's reaction was exactly opposite to that. His arguments in this speech were simply careless and entirely beside the point, and they show no reason for his subsequent emotional and dogged opposition to Lenin. The reason for that was his passionate and loyal devotion to the solidarity of "Iskra." If he had not had that feeling, which was essentially a feeling for organization and not an individualistic feeling, he would never have been carried out of his course—the course indicated by his own previous speeches and articles in "Iskra"—by the mere accident of personal association. And if he had not had in his mind, all through the years of his political isolation, his notorious "standing alone," the idea and the belief that the true party consisted of the sincere revolutionists in both these groups, he would not have stood alone. His position was one of stubborn loyalty to the true party as he erroneously but realistically conceived it—the party which would actually unite and actually lead the revolution.

It is noticeable that more than once at this convention Lenin spoke immediately after Trotsky, and although he had older and weightier authorities to deal with he gave his best arguments in answer to this youth. And he always answered him gently, too, and very *teachingly*.

Indeed, I don't know any better way in which to teach the reader what he ought to know about the origin of Bolshevism than by quoting a passage from one of Lenin's answers to Trotsky:

"Coming now to the essence of the matter, I will say that Comrade Trotsky . . . missed the nub of the whole question. He talked of the intelligentsia and the workers, the class point of view and the mass movement, but failed to consider one fundamental point: Does my formula broaden or narrow the conception of a party member? If he had put himself that question, he might easily have seen that my formula narrows the conception, and Martov's broadens it, being distinguished (as Martov himself truly said) by 'elasticity.' Now it is exactly 'elasticity,' in such a period of party life as this we are living through, which opens the door for all kinds of dispersing, wavering and opportunistic elements. . . .

"The root mistake of those who stand for the formula of Comrade Martov consists in their ignoring one of the prime evils of our party life, and not only ignoring but glorifying it. That evil consists in this: That in an atmosphere of almost universal political dissatisfaction and under conditions of complete secrecy in our work, the concentration of the greater part of our activity in narrow underground circles and even personal conversations, it is to the last degree difficult and well-nigh impossible to distinguish the gabblers from the workers. . . . Better that ten workers should not call themselves members of the party (real workers are not so eager for position) than that one gabbler should have the right and the opportunity to be a party member. There is the principle which seems to me irrefutable, and which compels me to fight against Martov. . . ."

Lenin was forming a party of leaders, the vanguard of a revolutionary class, and he knew by some natural miracle of wisdom that more than half of those who offered themselves for membership would be waging war against him when the day of action came. He knew moreover that Trotsky would not. That was why he concentrated such a wealth of fatherly-spoken counsel upon him in the convention. And that was why, when Trotsky went for some months into the camp of the Mensheviks, Lenin never lost confidence in him, never broke with him, as he did with everyone who he believed had really gone over, consciously or unconsciously, to the side of the enemy.

And through all the long years when Trotsky stood between the two "factions," trying boldly and foolishly to unite them and saying many injurious and erroneous things about Lenin's policy, Lenin never responded to him in a way that would seriously injure his prestige. He never ceased to believe in him. He never ceased to love him with the confident admiration of a comrade in arms. Trotsky received a letter from Lenin's wife the week after Lenin died, which testifies to the personal side of this assertion.

"And I want to tell you this," she said, "the relation which was formed between Vladimir Ilych and you, when you came to us in London from Siberia, never changed with him to the day of his death."

That the political accord between Lenin and Trotsky was also as close at the end as it was at the beginning of their friendship, is known to everybody who has access to political information in Moscow. Lenin offered to Trotsky, when he first fell sick, the position of acting head of the government, which was subsequently given—because of Trotsky's own decision—to Rykov. Three times during his illness Lenin appealed to Trotsky to defend his policies in the party executive in opposition to an opposing group. Once he appealed to him to compel the party organ, "Pravda," to publish an article of his which they withheld because it fiercely criticized one of the institutions organized by this group—an article that has since become a guiding document for the party. And in the weeks preceding his last serious illness Lenin wrote a letter to the party convention, shrewdly characterizing the different party leaders and expressly designating Trotsky as the man in whom he had the most confidence when faced with the prospect of his own death.

THE END